OVERWHELMED

OVERWHELMED

Coping with Life's Ups and Downs

SECOND EDITION

NANCY K. SCHLOSSBERG

M. Evans

Lanham • New York • Boulder • Toronto • Plymouth, UK

Published by M. Evans
An imprint of The Rowman & Littlefield Publishing Group, Inc.
4501 Forbes Boulevard, Suite 200, Lanham, Maryland 20706

Estover Road, Plymouth PL6 7PY, United Kingdom

Distributed by NATIONAL BOOK NETWORK

Library of Congress Cataloging-in-Publication Data

Schlossberg, Nancy K., 1929-
  Overwhelmed : coping with life's ups and downs / Nancy K. Schlossberg. — 2nd ed.
    p. cm.
  Includes bibliographical references and index.
  ISBN-13: 978-1-59077-126-6 (pbk. : alk. paper)
  ISBN-10: 1-59077-126-5 (pbk. : alk. paper)
  1. Change (Psychology) 2. Life change events. 3. Change (Psychology)—Case studies. 4. Life change events—Case studies. I. Title.
  BF637.C4S35 2008
  158.1—dc22

                                                                2007018494

Manufactured in the United States of America.

To my granddaughters, who give me great joy and strength to face whatever lies ahead; Robin, age four, and Jennie Rose, age two; and to Charlie Tolchin who dealt with life's blows, facing death all through his young life, with courage and equanimity. They are my inspiration.

CONTENTS

Acknowledgments

Jason Hallman, my editor for the Lexington Books edition of *Overwhelmed*, supported my efforts to find another publisher once Lexington moved exclusively into the textbook business. He sent my work to Camille Cline, then acquisitions editor at Taylor Trade Publishing. We immediately connected. Working with her on the new edition has been a pleasure.

Two interns from New College, Sarasota, Florida—Heather A. King and Lisa N. Harrington—simplified the library research. For example, Heather uncovered all the newest references on resilience, which I have built into the text, and Lisa clarified the research on work-life fit and work-life balance. Their help was enormous.

My colleague and dear friend, Stephanie Kay, is always there giving me support. She encouraged me to incorporate the Transition Guide, our joint product, as the final chapter of the book.

Betty Bowers, secretary and friend, helps in countless ways, the most important of which is the commitment she shows to my various projects. She typed the original manuscript in 1989 and is on board again in 2005. Modern technology makes it essential to have a computer guru on hand. Tudor Stefan Popescu, assistant administrator at the Cosmos Club in Washington, DC, continually helped me with computer problems, making it possible to produce this book. Thanks to the continued support given by the colleagues with whom

I have worked over the years. The assistance given by Richard Chapman, Karen Samuelsen, and Jun Li is greatly appreciated.

Many thanks to my friends, Norma Sue Madden and Marcia Weiss, who have supported me since junior high school days as I cope with personal and professional transitions; and to my husband, Steve, and adult children, Karen and Mark, with whom I share the joys and sorrows that are part of the adult years.

I am especially grateful to those who shared their life stories with me, which showed their enormous resources to manage change, teaching me that "the best is yet to be."

PREFACE

Why write a new edition of *Overwhelmed?* In 1989, when it was originally published, Google did not exist, 9/11 meant nothing, Internet dating was unheard of, talking on cell phones on every street corner was nonexistent, househusbands were hardly a blip on the landscape, and the issue of grandparents raising grandchildren—four million of them—was not addressed.

We have survived an overwhelming attack on our security, many have faced job loss, there is no longer the assurance that working hard and being loyal to the company will result in promotions, most families no longer have the opportunity to choose to work or stay at home, and an increasing number of people cannot afford health insurance. Furthermore, the Internet has changed our lives. In addition to instant communication, people are falling in love over the Internet. In short, people are facing new challenges as they try to balance work and family, loyalty to a workplace and loyalty to themselves. As sociologist Phyllis Moen wrote, "Millions of Americans . . . [have] too much to do and too little time to do it, often with the need and desire to be at two places at once."[1] As one young woman said, "I wish I could clone myself. I need to be two people."

I remember the overwhelming pressures I felt when working full time as a professor, raising two children with my husband Steve, and caring for two parents when each was terminally ill, thinking, "If I am having such stress, what about people who do not have secure jobs with pensions, what about the single parent, recently divorced, with little financial resources, but with family obligations?"

The pressures people experience—in all walks of life—require a new look at *Overwhelmed: Coping with Life's Ups and Downs*. No matter where I went, I heard stories of people feeling pushed to the limits. Whether it is the woman supporting a family of four on limited income; the single parent by choice; the man supporting and physically caring for his mother and disabled sister; the retired professor suddenly thrust into caring for grandchildren; the writer dealing with rejection; the friend not understanding why a relationship has dissolved; the lover of sixty years putting his wife in a nursing home; women feeling pressure to be "perfect moms," work performers, and attentive lovers; the woman who discovers her husband has been having an Internet affair with a "bimbo" whom he later marries—these and others highlight the universal feeling of being overwhelmed.

The ability to tackle this, to handle it, to turn it into an opportunity is what is crucial—now more than ever. So the decision to update *Overwhelmed* was made. *Overwhelmed* is a book that is unique in the way it helps people make sense out of the enormous transitions they face in everyday life. It is the only book on transitions that is based on years of research—studies of people moving, adults returning to school, people whose jobs were eliminated, retirement, non-events like not having a baby or not getting promoted, and so on. These studies resulted in the development of a generic framework for understanding any type of transition. Based on this research, *Overwhelmed* presents a step-by-step approach to turning overwhelming transitions into challenging experiences. By systematically sizing up transitions and one's resources for dealing with them, people can learn how to build on their strengths, cut their losses, and even grow in the process. In other words, this book is more than inspirational. It provides a person with tools for understanding and action. In summary, my work on transitions provides a systematic approach to any transition that is based on a theoretical framework but written in everyday language.

The basic model that takes the mystery—not the misery—out of change remains the same. There are new cases and many sections have been expanded. There is a new chapter on non-events. The final chapter, "It's Your Turn Now," includes the Transition Guide, which helps identify your resources for coping with life's ups and downs. I hope these additions will enhance your understanding of your own transitions, offering clues to more creative coping.

INTRODUCTION

- A woman finds a great job in the city where her lover lives. A year after she relocates she wonders, "Why am I so depressed?"
- After being forced to retire, a man feels his life lacks purpose. Angry at the company and himself, he keeps asking, "Is this all there is?"
- "I am a dumpee," says a woman whose husband of thirty-five years left her for another woman. "I feel like a discarded rag. How will I ever get my life back together?"
- A young man gently cradling his exhausted wife in the delivery room tells her, "He's perfect. He's ours. We're a family at last."
- "How will I construct a life without Al? After fifty years of marriage, he was my life." Even after two years of being widowed, Marge cannot regain her sense of joy and purpose.

All of us face transitions or turning points in our lives. Wondering how to handle these journeys, live through them, and learn from them is what this book is about.

Many years ago, my husband and I decided that it was time to move. We planned the move carefully and managed to find jobs in another city where we had friends, colleagues, and children as stabilizing elements. Yet I was depressed for two years after moving. Why wasn't I weathering this change I had sought? Why was it so hard?

This experience prompted me to remember many other changes I had experienced in the past. I found it perplexing that in some instances I had coped successfully and felt like the rock of Gibraltar, while in others I had felt as if I might shatter. As I thought about other people who had experienced transitions like retirement, job change, and family change, I realized that they had also reacted differently, over time, to the same kinds of transitions. I began to search for ways to make sense out of how people cope with life's ups and downs.

I asked my friend, Dr. Sue M. Smock, a sociologist, whether it was possible to develop a system that would be helpful to people in *any* kind of transition. Sue suggested a way to start: List all the factors that could possibly make a difference in how one copes with change. This list became the basis for my studies of people in transition. With different colleagues, I studied the experiences of people who were going through different types of transitions: men whose jobs had been eliminated, clerical workers who faced job and family changes, adult learners who were returning to school, couples who had moved geographically, adults who were caring for aging parents, people dealing with non-event transitions, and retirees finding new paths.

As a result of these studies—and others designed by scholars studying the adult years—I developed a structured approach that extends the ways people handle transitions and provides a road map for managing any change.

This is where you come in. Are you thinking about changing jobs, partners, or lifestyles? Are you beset by changes you don't expect or want? Have you learned the hard way that times of transition are some of the most difficult in life? Are you excited about the possibility of a new relationship? Are you wondering whether to take early retirement? Do you really believe that adjustment to new conditions, good or bad, can be very difficult? Are you overwhelmed? If the answer is yes, this book can be of special help to you. It provides not just text, not just a theory, but an organized series of activities to help you gain control of your life. That means acquiring a new perspective on transitions, and developing strategies for dealing with them.

Overwhelmed: Coping with Life's Ups and Downs won't tell you how to fix old houses, flabby thighs, shaky bank accounts, or a turbulent love life. It doesn't promise spectacular results in ten minutes or even ten days. What it does is offer a way to think about some of the most challenging issues you now face and are likely to encounter in the years to come. In a nutshell, it tells you how to cope more effectively with the important changes in your life. I call these changes *transitions.*

Transitions are the changes—good or bad, expected or unexpected—that unsettle us. They may be prompted by a host of incidents—a move to a new city, a lost promotion, a new baby, the death of someone close, a financial windfall, an incapacitating accident or illness. These are things that can and do happen to everyone—male or female, rich or poor, young or old, black or white. Yet surprisingly, most people understand very little about transitions or how to manage them creatively.

Every day people face transitions in their lives that are as taxing psychologically as marathons are physically. And they do this with little or no training or preparation. Small wonder they're often exhausted and overwhelmed. This need not be.

I'm convinced that even someone already in the beginning or middle of a transition can learn to meet the challenges with grace, skill, and mastery. That's why I wrote this book. In it I present steps for you to APPROACH, TAKE STOCK, and TAKE CHARGE of a transition—any transition—so you can master it. As you will see, the book is organized around these steps:

- Part I, "APPROACHING CHANGE," lays the foundation so that you can understand your particular transition.
- Part II, "TAKING STOCK," centers on your own resources and outlines a procedure that will enable you to assess your

resources for coping—what I call your 4 S's: *Situation, Self, Supports, Strategies.*

- Part III shifts the focus to your own plan, with a suggested procedure for TAKING CHARGE and profiting from change.

Cases of real people (though not their actual names) are used throughout the book to illustrate the system's use in any situation. You can diagnose your coping resources and assess whether your balance of resources at this time makes the possibility of a change look feasible. If there are too many negatives, then you can introduce some strategies to strengthen your coping resources, enabling you to initiate the change at a more appropriate time. If you are weathering change, you can go through the same process—assess your coping resources, see what needs bolstering, and then use your coping strategies to help you handle this difficult time with more options, understanding, and control.

First, I examine what is common to all adults—the fact that they experience transitions, what those transitions are, and how they change our lives. We cannot predict when someone will marry, divorce, retire, or return to school, but we can say with certainty that all of us will experience and probably require some help in getting through transitions.

Second, having explored the commonalities and the differences in many types of transitions, I offer a method for coping with change systematically. That means all changes. This is not a one-solution recipe for change, but rather a method of arriving at the solution that is appropriate for you.

Third, this book integrates what is known from scholars and researchers into an understandable, practical package without requiring the reader to wade through many pages of technical jargon.

Fourth, this is not a substitute for seeking professional help from a counselor, psychologist, social worker, psychiatrist, psychoanalyst, or member of the clergy. I believe that there are situations in which we do need professional help, and reading this book may assist you to decide for yourself if and when it's necessary.

Fifth, the case histories—real stories—generously distributed throughout the book will show you how others handle the problems, challenges, and opportunities associated with change. You may not find a case that is the mirror image of your own, but you can gain confidence and competence as a result of these stories. You will begin to see that there is a structure for dealing with any life change. You will have at hand a system that can galvanize your will and energy for handling change, predict your readiness for change, measure your resources for dealing with changes that have occurred, and offer new strategies to make you more effective and creative in willing and weathering change.

Transitions are part and parcel of adult life. And so is the discomfort they can cause. They can disrupt your capacity to love, work, and play. But transitions needn't be overwhelming. You can master your own transitions by understanding the transition process, recognizing and harnessing your own considerable coping strengths and skills, and selectively adding new ones.

YOUR STEPS IN MASTERING CHANGE

Approaching Change
- Identify your transition:
    What it is
    How it has changed your roles, routines, assumptions, relationships
    The transition process: where you are

Taking Stock
- Assess your potential resources for coping with your transition:
    Your four S's—your *Situation, Self, Supports,* and *Strategies*

Taking Charge
- Strengthen your coping resources by selecting appropriate coping strategies
- Develop an action plan
    Profit from change: increase your options, understanding, and control

I

APPROACHING CHANGE

This section answers the question "If only I had known then what I know now." How often have you said or heard this expression? I use it here because it sums up the importance of being able to predict, anticipate, and understand our life transitions. The need for predictability in life may explain the popularity of so-called stage theories that assign certain characteristics to each phase of our lives, implying that you are doomed to live through these chronological phases.

But in the absence of such certainty about the timing and types of transitions we will face, we must be satisfied with knowing that we will all experience both events and non-events continually; and that by strengthening the ability to understand them and by exercising coping skills, we will be better prepared to master the transitions and not allow them to control us.

All of us have periods when everything seems fine: we work, play, love, and don't think too much about it. But then change may intrude in our lives and make us feel "out of sync." Suddenly we are taking a personal inventory, thinking about who we are and where we're going. We may face a crisis of confidence or competence.

Many report that when they go through transitions, they become self-centered. When they realize that it is perfectly normal to soul-search at times of transition, they express relief. I have learned to expect stock-taking and soul-searching whenever change occurs.

This section provides basic information about transitions that will be your foundation for APPROACHING CHANGE. Chapter 1 describes the dynamic process included in any transition; chapter 2 describes the different types of transitions that surface. This knowledge is crucial as you move toward your goal of taking control and profiting from change.

1

THE TRANSITION PROCESS

"Now what?" "What next?" These lifelong questions crop up with every transition and challenge all of us. We know that each person experiences many transitions, many crises. Let's start our understanding of change with some definitions.

TRANSITIONS: A DEFINITION

When we think about transitions in our lives, the ones most likely to come to mind are the noteworthy events that happen to us, expectedly or unexpectedly. But some equally important transitions stem from "non-events," the things we expect and hope for that somehow fail to happen, such as *not* being able to have a baby, or *not* getting a promotion. Both kinds of transitions can bring considerable change. The significance of the event or non-event lies in how and to what extent it alters our lives.

We must be cautious about judging the severity of an event simply by labeling it. A transition that is severe for one person may be relatively minor for another, depending on the degree to which it alters the person's *roles, relationships, routines,* and *assumptions.*

The following clues will help you determine the significance of a particular transition:

Clue 1. How has the transition changed your *roles?* For example, you have a baby, and suddenly you've become a parent; you change jobs, and you take on a whole new set of responsibilities. All of us enact many *roles* in life. We are friends, parents, children, coworkers, employees, employers, neighbors, students, teachers, and much more, depending on the circumstances. And in each of these *roles,* we have particular *relationships* with our family and others around us.

Examples of transitions that can change our *roles* include divorce, having a child or a grandchild, seeing our children grow up and leave home, moving into a better job or losing a job, graduating from college, or undertaking a new career in middle age. A divorce means that we lose a partnership and the role of spouse, and it can also mean that we lose neighbors and sometimes friends. The same is true when we lose a job. When we change jobs and are required to make a move, we lose neighbors and friends and perhaps group membership, but we gain a new *role* in the workforce.

In analyzing a transition, it is useful to delineate the role changes. Which are gains and which are losses? Even if we gain new roles in the course of a change, the more *roles* that are altered, the more we have to adapt. We must remember that with *role* changes come changes in *routines,* in *relationships,* and in *assumptions.*

Clue 2. How has the transition changed your *relationships?* For example, being a parent puts you in touch with new people, as does a new job. Both experiences also transform your existing relationships. Having your colleague become your boss will change your relationship. You are no longer on equal footing. Many retirees report that their relationships with former colleagues change dramatically. The daily camaraderie no longer exists. This illustrates the interaction of changed *roles* leading to changed *relationships*.

Clue 3. How has the transition changed your *routines?* For example, a new baby alters living and sleeping habits; a new job may require a shift in schedule and in commuting patterns.

Some of us do not realize the importance of routines in our daily life until they are changed or eliminated. Even minor *routines*—taking a coffee break with a coworker who is a valued friend or watching the news every night at seven o'clock—provide us with an important measure of serenity, solace, and comfort.

In one case, a widow and mother of three children married a man with three children of his own. She expected *role* changes, especially when the whole family moved into her house. She acquired not only a husband and a larger family but the *role* of stepparent, which brought with it a changed *relationship* with her former in-laws and a new *relationship* with her new in-laws.

She had expected to undergo some difficulty with her *role* changes, but the additional difficulties of adjusting to new daily *routines* came as a surprise. All the logistical and mechanical issues of daily life—who makes the beds, who washes the dishes, who drives the carpool, who shops and cooks—suddenly had to be renegotiated. In another case, a woman and her children moved in with her new husband and his children. As the husband said, "The forks and knives were no longer in their 'right place.'"

Some people regard changes in *routine* as positive. For example, one writer who moved from New York City to France basked in her change of *routine*. She said, "I found it easier to change *almost* everything at once—where I lived, what I ate, how I exercised, my work routine—when I went to France. Sometimes I have felt jarred when my *routines* change, but because I was seeking change, this time it was exhilarating." It is not the *amount* of *role* or *routine* change that is the primary factor in how we weather a transition—it is how we evaluate it.

Clue 4. How has the transition affected your *assumptions* about yourself and the world? I often lead transition workshops during which I ask participants which changes are most difficult. The answer is often the same: events that change one's definition of oneself. One participant held an important job, but she was frightened by the responsibility. It took about a year for her to realize that she could not only do the job but do it well. She eventually defined herself as someone who is comfortable with being in control. In another, less happy case, a man who lost his job and could not find another began to see himself as worthless and therefore unemployable. Or a new father discovers he's more protective and responsible than he thought he would be, or a person in a new secretarial position may discover personal strengths and weaknesses that went unrecognized in the old clerk-typist job.

If a transition is major, it will change all four aspects of your life: your *roles*, *relationships*, *routines*, and *assumptions*. If it changes only one or two, it is still a transition, but clearly one of less magnitude.

The same type of transition, such as retirement, can affect people in very different ways. One person may view it as a very positive change—the gateway to a new career or a new life of leisure; another may view it as a very negative one—a one-way ticket to limbo.

Further, what appears to be the same transition may be a major trauma for one person but a minor problem for someone else. Consider, for example, the lives of two clerical workers, Adrienne and Bette, each of whom took responsibility for caring for an aging parent.

For Adrienne, almost everything in her life was altered after her mother—already frail—broke her hip. She had always been dependent on her mother, but now her mother depended on her; Adrienne's *role* had changed. Her *relationships* with her own family were changing as well. She had little time for her husband and children since so much of her time was spent caring for her mother. Her *routines* were clearly changed. Instead of going home after work, she went right to her mother's house, where she spent almost six hours each day until her brother came to relieve her. Only her *assumptions* about herself were unaltered. She had always considered herself a devoted daughter, and caring for her mother now was consistent with that image.

Bette, also a devoted daughter, was faced with an apparently similar situation, but in reality it was quite different. In Bette's family her sister was the main caregiver. Her mother and sister both felt that Bette should do more, but she had small children and refused to disrupt her own family. So although her *role* and *routines* were not upset nearly as much as Adrienne's were, her *assumptions* about herself were much more in flux; she felt guilty much of the time.

The outward transition may look the same, but only the person involved can define whether the transition is positive or negative and the degree to which one's life has been altered. Even a positive and not-very-disruptive transition requires a period of adjustment.

TODAY IS NOT FOREVER

Although the onset of a transition may be linked to one identifiable event, transitions take time. Six months, a year, sometimes two years pass before one moves fully through a major transition. Realizing this makes it possible to be kinder to oneself and more understanding to friends who have difficulty coping with change.

Often our first reaction to a transition is extreme, possibly very emotional. Have you ever been jilted? I have. The day of the Big Jilt, I was devastated and thought I would never recover. Within a year, I was happily involved with someone new.

I have interviewed men who lost their jobs because of a plant closing. They, too, felt that they would never recover. Art said, "I feel as if I have been hit on the head and kicked in the back. I will never get over it." But six months later he was in a new job and could joke about his earlier desperation. Not all transitions end so well. Another man in this group who failed to find a job was still depressed six months after the layoff.

At first you are consumed by the change, preoccupied with thinking and talking about it. This is followed by a middle period of disruption—a period of great vulnerability. You're likely to experience confusion about what to do next, how to behave. Tiny details can become problematic. If, for example, you have just moved in with someone, it takes a while to know where the dishes and glasses are stored. But more important, it takes time to feel comfortable rearranging them. Finally, the change becomes integrated into your life, for better or worse. You've accommodated to your transition. Your former *roles*, *routines*, *relationships*, and *assumptions* have been replaced by new ones.

Time transforms some bad events, but it also alters good ones. One day you marry the person of your dreams or connect with the love of your life and decide to move in together. You think, "I will always feel like this. Nothing will ever come between us." Yet, a few months or years later you may have a major blowup and wonder what you ever saw in this person.

In order to illustrate the different ways transitions can change lives, I will relate the stories of five people: Carolyn, a newlywed; Warren, who cared first for his mother and, after her death, for his sister; Cathy, one of the first women appointed to a highly responsible executive position; and Melissa and Frank, who moved from their family home into a condominium apartment. First, the story of Carolyn.

Carolyn the Newlywed

In fairy tales, princesses marry princes, ride off into the sunset, and live happily ever after. In real life, even if people do manage to live happily, it can take quite a bit of adjusting to get to "ever after." Carolyn, for example, married her high school sweetheart and moved with him from Cleveland into a small town.

We interviewed Carolyn right after her move. She said, "If you had a ten-point scale and ten was miserable, I'd be off the scale." Back home she had been part of a tightly knit religious group and had had the support of many close friends and relatives. In her new community she felt isolated. Her husband needed the car to go to work, and lacking convenient transportation, Carolyn stayed in their apartment, without friends or support. To add to her dismay during this lonely period, she had the discomfort and disappointment of a tubal pregnancy.

In an interview six months later, Carolyn sounded very different. She had worked to overcome her isolation and was making some headway. After negotiating the use of the car, she joined a religious group similar to the one in her hometown and even started a newcomers' club. She had also arranged regular phone chats with family and friends in her old community. "I'd still rather be back home," she said, but she no longer felt like a complete outsider and was beginning to build a new circle of friends.

Carolyn's story shows that when you reflect on how you felt at the beginning of a transition and compare it with your feelings about it later, it's evident that a transition does not happen only at one given point in time. Rather, it is a process—an episode with a beginning, a middle, and usually an end. And all through the transition, your reactions and emotions continue to change as you integrate the event or nonevent into your life.

Warren the Caregiver

Warren, a sixty-three-year-old divorced man, who has had open heart surgery, was principal caregiver for his eighty-three-year-old mother until she died, and is now totally in charge of his fifty-year-old disabled sister. He was forced out of a job because he was constantly leaving work to take his mother to the emergency room or do something for his sister. He rarely sleeps through the night and his life consists of constant crises. Despite the stress, Warren said, "I am proud to being doing this. This was the right thing with no regrets.

My mom did so much for me when I was growing up. . . . I'm doing what I hope my daughter would do for me."

Warren feels as if his life is on hold—that he cannot make any personal plans. All he can do is go to work, come home, and take care of his sister. He is trying to figure out a better solution.

Cathy the Executive

Consider the example of Cathy, who was recently promoted to a top executive position—one of the first women to fill this role. At first, the newspaper articles about her thrilled Cathy and her family; she could think of nothing else. But now that she has been in the job for three weeks, she is beginning to feel very confused. The excitement is over, and she is not sure how to behave, how to feel. Cathy is particularly bothered by her new role supervising her former colleagues; she feels isolated from them. The very people she's normally leaned on for support are now the ones she's supposed to lead, evaluate, and even fire if need be. This is her vulnerable period, one that can last from a week to several years. If she adjusts well, she will become used to her new role and its power and even come to enjoy it. If she does not, she will suffer, lose confidence, become depressed, and perhaps seek another, less stressful job.

Whether the transition turns out for better or worse, it is still a slow process during which *roles*, *relationships*, *routines*, and *assumptions* keep changing.

Melissa and Frank: The Moving Family

Melissa and Frank realized that their house needed extensive repairs, and their son was a senior in high school preparing to attend college. With a minimal amount of soul-searching, they decided to sell their home. Thrilled when they were quickly offered the asking price, they moved to an apartment building that allowed dogs, and proceeded to invest in major redesign.

Before moving in, they were concerned about three issues: Would they fit into the space? Would the renovations be finished in time? Would their son adjust? They felt they could handle anything. After all, they had elected this transition, and they saw themselves as creative copers.

The complaints started the day they moved into the apartment. Their dog, the construction, and their teenage son all became subjects of a neighbor's gripes to the manager. Even though the "best" dog trainer in the city pronounced their dog normal and the neighbors in need of training, Melissa still felt guilty and anxious every time the dog was left alone in the apartment. Petty accusations increased—their son walked through the lobby without a shirt. Melissa and Frank felt as if they had been suddenly transformed from desirable neighbors into pariahs. They did not want to move back to a big house, but they wondered if they could ever learn to tolerate "condominium mentality."

As time went on, they began to enjoy the condo and all its resources, but even then it seemed that every time they relaxed, something else went wrong. They were amazed by the amount of adjustment this elected transition required. One day Melissa was in tears about the move. She realized that this was a process and though she might be overwhelmed at the beginning, they would eventually incorporate it into their lives.

As they looked back they realized that their move was a process that started with excitement about the move, then went through shock about the complaints, soul-searching about whether they had made the right decision, and—finally—contentment with the move. Eventually, they were delighted to live where they do. Their son moved to his own apartment nearby, and they no longer care about complaints from neighbors.

Many who write about the transition process suggest that people go through sequentially specific stages from beginning to end. In fact, they give labels to each stage. My research and experience lead me to conclude that life is not that orderly. The labels don't work. What I have found is the following: If the transition is major (having altered your *roles*, *relationships*, *routines*, and *assumptions*), you will be consumed with it at the beginning. Then you will experience a middle period, during which you will learn the ropes but still feel vulnerable. Eventually you will incorporate the transition into your life, as Melissa and Frank did. They rarely think about the move now, although on occasion they miss the informal atmosphere of a house. On balance they have concluded that the benefits outweigh the losses. Reactions to good and bad transitions change over time, and an important factor in APPROACHING CHANGE is recognizing that we need time to adjust.

APPROACHING CHANGE: A PERSPECTIVE

There are a number of assumptions embedded in this approach. One is that transitions can be either positive or negative, but if they have altered your life in significant ways, you will need to cope. The more your life is altered, the more you will have to bring your coping resources to bear on the change. Even if members of a group appear to be in the same boat—as we saw with the job loss group—each has unique problems that require unique solutions.

APPROACHING CHANGE requires knowing what change is, how you appraise it, and how much it has altered your life. The next chapter describes the multiple types of change you will encounter—an important aspect of APPROACHING CHANGE.

YOUR TRANSITION

Name the Transition that is currently uppermost in your life.

Rate the degree to which your Transition changed your life on a 3-point scale: 1 is very little and 3 is very much.

Has it changed your *roles?*
Has it changed your *relationships?*
Has it changed your *routines?*
Has it changed your *assumptions?*

2

TRANSITIONS: THEIR INFINITE VARIETY

Some transitions are exciting, wonderful changes we never expected. Others we dream about for many years before finally taking the plunge and making them happen. Still others are sad losses that—expectedly or unexpectedly—alter our world. Since all of us dream of doing things that will change our lives, this section will start with a discussion of elected transitions: the ones we choose.

ELECTED TRANSITIONS

Some elected transitions are ones that are part of our culture—our social milestones—and others are ones we choose. Let's look more closely at examples of these two types of chosen changes: social milestones and individual choices.

Social Milestones

Many of the transitions in our lives are ones we initiate. We have been brought up to expect—and elect—certain transitions because they are major events in the lives of most people in our society. These social milestones include graduating from high school, moving away from home, getting your first real job, marrying, having a baby, and retiring. Not everyone chooses to experience all these transitions, but many people do, and there is strong social pressure to do so.

As transitions go, social milestones are cushioned for us in a number of ways. Because these events are expected, we usually have time to plan and rehearse for them. And there is usually an abundant supply of role models to show and tell us how to handle them. In addition, as we enter these transitions, we often get a helping hand from members of our community who celebrate our change in status.

Even though we expect to experience certain transitions in our lives, we still have difficulty since any change, even elected, alters our *roles*, *relationships*, *routines*, and *assumptions*. In addition, the fact that these transitions are common doesn't mean that everyone experiences them in the same ways. A few examples should make this very clear.

Jane has just graduated from high school. Graduation was an expected transition, and her school and family helped her make plans to go to college after graduation. But she did not feel ready to grow up. In fact, she stopped studying during her final semester, ending with a grade point average below C. The admissions counselor at the only college that had accepted her called to say they needed to rethink her admission; she wouldn't be allowed to start in the fall. She has left high school, but she does not really know what is next.

Most of her friends handled this transition quite differently. They graduated with reasonably good grades, found summer jobs to help pay for tuition, and despite some trepidation are looking forward to entering college in the fall. For them, high school graduation is an exciting opportunity to take the next step in life. But for Jane it is a threat; she resents being pressured to grow up and move out of her family's home.

Retirement illustrates another example of social milestones. When I compared the contents of interviews with newly retired people and recent high school graduates, an interesting point emerged. Despite the different issues facing each group, both were trying to figure out how to "get a life." Both had a strong sense of being in between who they were and who they were becoming.

This was highlighted when Zandy Leibowitz and I ran a workshop for partners and their spouses who were about to retire and some retired partners from a large accounting firm. The firm had an unwritten policy that required everyone to retire at age sixty, despite legislation eliminating age as a factor in retirement policies. During the two days we spent with them, it was clear that they were now facing what they knew was inevitable: giving up an immensely important part of the life they had known and valued for many years.

We discussed how this expected transition was likely to change their lives. As one wife said, "I don't think Don realizes how important his relationships at work have been. What will he substitute for them?"

One former partner who had retired two years earlier reported his surprise and dismay when he returned to the firm to have lunch with an active partner and realized that the partner viewed the occasion as a duty. For the retired partner, the biggest shift was the transition from being needed—indeed, central to the success of the company—to being marginal, even an annoyance. He hadn't yet found a new place to anchor his identity.

Another retired partner saw retirement in a different light. He had recently remarried and was thrilled at having much more time to spend with his new wife, get to know her family, and fashion a new life with her.

Thus a social milestone, whether it is high school graduation, retirement, or any other major expected event, is intrinsically neither good nor bad. It marks the end of one episode of life and the beginning of another. For those who focus on what is ending, it can be a threatening change. For those who focus on it as a beginning, it is an opportunity to explore and conquer new worlds.

Individual Choices

Other elected changes include individual choices that are outside the social timetable and are therefore more idiosyncratic. Some of these choices, such as shifting jobs or moving, are commonplace; they are generally socially condoned, as long as we don't hop around so often that we seem inordinately restless or unstable. Other individual choices, such as separating from a spouse, moving back into your parents' home, or changing religious affiliations, may even run counter to the prevailing social norms. Nevertheless, we sometimes choose such changes when it looks as if they may somehow improve our lives or at least make them less difficult.

Let's look at Paul Gauguin, who abandoned his career as a Parisian stockbroker to devote himself to being a painter in the idyllic setting of Tahiti. As he once wrote to his friend, Swedish playwright August Strindberg, "You suffer from your civilization. My barbarism is to me a renewal of my youth."

Why does Gauguin's story have such appeal? Maybe it touches our secret dreams of starting out fresh. Almost all of us respond in some way to news stories of men and women who shed their lovers and their jobs to take off in an entirely new direction.

Few people actually abandon all their ties to the past. But at certain points in life many people do choose new jobs, new communities, or new loves. Let's consider a few examples of the kinds of individual choices people make.

One day Terry, an editor in a publishing house, sent a letter to one of his clients, who was writing a book on midlife. "Dear Jean, I have enjoyed working with you on the book. As you know, I think it is a real winner. In fact, it is so good that I have taken it to heart and am writing to tell you that I have resigned from the company; I am leaving publishing and am opening a boutique in Carmel. As I was working on your manuscript, I kept thinking, 'What about my life? Is this really how I want to spend it? Isn't there more to life than editing other people's manuscripts?' As you can see, I decided to give it a try and change gears. Thank you for inspiring me to take the leap, and good luck to you."

Lisa also shifted gears but in a different way. Recently relocated from Omaha to Atlanta, she had moved for several reasons. In general, she was ready for a change, but she also wanted to be geographically closer to her partner of many years; she had also found a good job there. In her new city she had a ready-made support system of friends, a house to move into, and a prestigious job. Nonetheless, when we had lunch about a year after her move, Lisa said she felt very confused and depressed. Since her relationship with her partner and her job were both working out pretty well, she couldn't understand why she felt this way.

Lisa didn't realize that although the change she initiated was a positive one, it still required many adjustments: daily life with her lover, a challenging new job, an unfamiliar city. She had been part of another world with set *relationships*, *roles*, *routines*, and *assumptions*. Now all these were changed. She hadn't foreseen how long it would take to learn the new "rules" and figure out where she fit in.

We often think that confusion and discomfort happen only in response to negative changes. But any major transition, even ones we dream about and freely choose, requires adjustment.

SURPRISE TRANSITIONS— WHEN THE UNEXPECTED HAPPENS

Although many of the transitions in our lives are ones we initiate, there are many we can never anticipate. In brief, they're surprises, both good and bad. Your closest friend is in a serious car accident. You're fired. You make a killing in the stock market. You're passed over for a key promotion. A major film studio buys the rights to your first novel. You find romance in your eighties.

If the unexpected happens, you're in for a surprise—and possibly a transition. Whether the surprise is terrible or delightful, it can tax you emotionally and challenge your coping skills. Here are a few examples:

Dolores the Rejected

After thirty-five years of marriage, Dolores's husband announced that he felt too young to "dry up"; he had fallen in love and was leaving to join the new woman in his life. What really stunned Dolores was that her husband had fallen in love with a woman his own age. She couldn't even rationalize his behavior as one of those midlife May–December flings. "It completely knocked me off my pins," she said. After two years of depression, she decided to return to school, where she is now getting a nursing degree. She is still angry and somewhat depressed, but as she puts it, "At least I'm working on something."

Bill's Second Chance

Bill, too, had been depressed for several years, but for a different reason. His thirty-year marriage was going strong, but he was very unhappy in his work life. He had taken early retirement from a high-level position in the United Nations—a job that required a great deal of political know-how and made him feel useful and important. Knowing he was not ready to quit working, he had joined a small consulting practice where his focus shifted from "saving the world" to "getting clients." He hated worrying about every "billable breath," but he felt that at age sixty-four, this was the best he could do. He would come home at about 4:30 every day, putter, and watch TV. Bill told his wife he felt like a "has-been." Several friends suggested therapy, but he resisted. He was a classical example of a man caught in an unsuccessful transition.

One day, out of the blue, Bill was offered a top position that enabled him to return to public service. He accepted it on the spot and left the consulting firm. The new job, he said, is "just what the doctor ordered." He has been rejuvenated. Although he now works twelve-hour days and is on a grueling travel schedule, he said, "I am the luckiest man in the world—at sixty-four to be given the chance to do an important job." He had taken a risk, but he was ready for it. "God willing, I plan to spend another ten years at it."

Bill's story is unusual in several respects. First, a totally unexpected opportunity made the real difference. Instead of spending the rest of his life in low gear, he is on the road, growing and contributing. Second, since he had never adjusted well to his consulting job, the shift back to a more familiar and congenial type of work was liberating, not disturbing. True, his *routines* are disrupted by lots of travel, but his *assumptions* about himself have been reinforced by his new job: he is a man who loves public service and who also has had the good fortune to find a second rewarding career.

Maggie's Unexpected Second Round of Parenting

Maggie, an employee with the United States Postal Service, was forced to take her five-year-old grandchild away from her son and daughter-in-law, both of whom were heavily into drugs. Maggie did not want to bring legal action against them, but she worried about what would happen if her son demanded his child back. Although she was stressed, she loved her granddaughter and was committed to bringing her up. In addition, she worried about what would happen if she died.

This transition is not one most grandparents expect. However, about 4.5 million children under eighteen are being raised by their grandparents. There are many reasons for this increase: parents are abusing drugs and alcohol, parents are incarcerated, parents neglect or abuse their children, and parents have died as a result of accidents or illness. Whatever the reason, these grandparents are experiencing a major change to a caregiving *role*, a major change of *routines* back to a schedule determined by a child, a changed *relationship* with one's adult child, and a changed set of *assumptions* about the way life is going to be lived.

NON-EVENTS: WHEN THE EXPECTED DOESN'T HAPPEN

We can be just as surprised when expected events don't happen as we are when unexpected ones do. The expected ones that fail to materialize—called *non-events*—can pack just as powerful a wallop in our lives.

For many, the non-event of infertility is major. When they finally realize that pregnancy will not occur, this non-event kicks off a transition. The impact of infertility is often much greater on women than on men. But once women accept the fact that they cannot have children, they begin to make different *assumptions* about their *relationships* and *roles*—especially their work roles. For example, one woman in the study had been coasting along on a series of low-level temporary jobs. But when medical tests confirmed that she could not become pregnant, she began to make plans to return to school and become a speech therapist.

Lost dreams can and do happen to everyone. In a series of studies, reported in *Going to Plan B: How You Can Cope, Regroup, and Start Your Life on a New Path*, Susan Porter Robinson and I described the variety of non-events people experience.[1] For example, people have expectations about their lives—about what will happen in their love and family life, their careers, and their personal development, and about the legacy they might leave. When these expectations are unmet, when their dreams are not realized, people can experience a feeling of heartbreak.

I was discussing the concept of non-events with Marshal, a graphic designer with whom I was working. He commented, "I have no time for non-events. I am running a business, caring for two children, dealing with parents and parents-in-laws. I am overwhelmed." A few minutes later he said, "I just realized my father is a walking non-event. At fifty he realized his career was going badly. He retired feeling like a failure. Now he tries to micromanage my business and life. His disappointments affect the rest of us."

Non-events come from many places. Some are personal, such as "I did not get the promotion I expected"; others ripple from someone else, like Marshal's; or non-events can result from an event such as the accident that resulted in a disability and stopped the person from leading the expected life. There are delayed non-events: For example, a woman thought she would never become a grandparent because her children did not have children. After many years, this non-event became an event. It was merely delayed.

Harry, the Chief Who Never Was

Non-events in our lives are often more difficult to handle than events. They are usually not public; others can't see them, and unlike many expected events—especially social milestones—there are rarely any rituals to help us cope with them. For example, the realization that one will never be promoted to a coveted position at work can alter a person's self-image and expectations for the future. Yet, one does not announce this transition to the world or mark it with a ritual. Here's how one person reacted to this non-event.

Harry had been waiting for years for a promotion to bureau chief at his newspaper. "At first," he said, "when I did not get my promotion, I thought it was because I was so young. As the years passed, I began to wonder: When? Finally, at age forty-five, I came across an article that explained that many organizations stop promoting people after they turn forty, and I suddenly realized that the answer to my question was Never! It was upsetting to realize that some people defined me as too old, even though I felt no different from what I was like in the past. I was not getting something I had always wanted. I blamed myself, and I blamed the system."

After wrestling for many months with his anger and frustration, Harry started to look for a new job, but he found nothing better than the one he already had. He then set his sights on a new goal: early retirement. Although he continued to perform his duties well, he stopped being a workaholic and started to see himself as "putting in time." Instead of working late and taking work home on weekends, he started using his free time to explore investment opportunities and new career paths that he might follow later.

Harry's non-promotion was a classic non-event and very painful at the time. But some non-events, like the one described below, can be opportunities.

Beth's Gift of Life

Beth was an active, vibrant woman who worked as a freelance writer. Her work, though emotionally and financially rewarding, was isolating and hard. When she learned she had a rare and fatal illness and had little time left to live, she gave up her career and decided to spend her last months being close to her children, bravely preparing to die. But to everyone's surprise and delight, Beth's illness remitted, and she lived. Strangely, even this almost miraculous turnabout was a transition and required adjustment. But she joyfully embraced the non-event and returned to her work as a writer. This time, though, she was less compulsive about work and built in more family time.

LIFE ON HOLD: THE TRANSITION WAITING TO HAPPEN

"Life on hold" is a transition waiting to happen, poised between an event and a non-event but really neither. For a variety of reasons, usually beyond your control, you can't bring about the change you want, but you haven't given up on it either. A few examples will show you what I mean.

Ted on Hold

Ted had always dreamed of being a journalist. After graduating from college, he landed a job as an editorial assistant at a national magazine. But he soon discovered that he had become a glorified clerk-typist, and the job was a bore. Although he was encouraged to write in his "spare" time and the magazine printed a number of his short articles, Ted still felt that he was wasting his time doing other people's "dog work" and that his plan to work his way up the organizational ladder was not panning out. Staff turnover at the magazine was rare, and he feared it would take forever to get a real writing position there. Ted was raring to leave.

When an exciting new magazine advertised for writers, Ted applied immediately and got exactly the job he had wanted. He was to start in a month. But during that month he started having strange physical symptoms and began a round of medical tests. No one could quite figure out what was wrong. Some doctors suggested it was "nerves," and others suggested a number of dire possibilities. He started some treatments, but they only made him feel worse. By the time he was to start the new job, he was embroiled in medical tests with indefinite results and lacked the energy to take on the challenge of the new venture.

Suddenly it wasn't so clear that he should leave the old job for the new one. Ted knew that he was valued in his old job and that he would have the support of his boss and office friends even if he took a lot of sick leave. He also had health insurance coverage for his mounting medical bills, but it wouldn't start at the new job until he had passed a three-month probationary period.

It was a heartbreaking decision, but he turned down the new job and put his career growth on hold. He decided to stay temporarily in his outgrown position and concentrate on finding someone who could diagnose and treat his puzzling disorder.

The Saga of Slow Shep

Vicky, like Ted, was working in her first job after college graduation. She had found a "dream" position in a prestigious design studio and had taken it even though it meant she'd be three hundred miles away from Shep, her lover, who was completing his graduate work. Since Shep had often talked about finding a job in her city after he got his degree, Vicky initially expected that they'd be separated only a year, until he graduated.

To overcome the strain of separation, Vicky and Shep called and wrote to each other regularly and maintained a commuting romance. Many of their weekends together were spent at the weddings of friends, who kidded them that they were "next." They both felt a growing sense of commitment to one another and at times talked about marriage, although they weren't engaged.

But then one year stretched to two, and Vicky began to worry that it might never lead to a long-term commitment. When Shep's dissertation was almost completed, he announced that he was start- ing to look for jobs in other cities as well as in hers. Vicky became angry. She felt it was time for them to live together and test their rela- tionship under conditions more normal than weekend trysts. Shep said that he felt the same way but that he didn't want to confine his job search to one city. When Vicky hinted that she'd give up her job and relocate if that was the only way they could be together, he said he couldn't ask her to do that, and it might not even be necessary if things worked out right.

Vicky feels caught in a bind. Her life is on hold. She feels too committed to Shep to date other people, but she cannot wait for him indefinitely, and she doesn't want to resort to "tricks" to make him join her. She has decided to back off from the issue of commitment and the crucial issue of the next step. There's a major transition in sight, but it's not clear yet whether it's a breakup or an engagement.

The Move That Never Happened

Jody married and moved to a small town in Virginia. She and her husband planned to move to New York City after they got established. On her sixtieth birthday she was in a deep funk. She realized that the move never would occur and that she would spend her days regretting their inaction. She felt her life had been wasted. Her husband pushed her into therapy so that she could put this in perspective. They faced the fact that they spent years deluding themselves about their move. As Jody said, "We decided to face our regrets and see how we could get part of our dream. We actually bought a timeshare in an apartment in New York City and now we go up twice a year for a week to shop, eat, and visit museums."

SLEEPER TRANSITIONS

Many transitions have an identifiable beginning point, such as a wedding, a move, or the death of a loved one. When they start, we're well aware that change is under way. But some transitions, called *sleepers*, start much more subtly and just creep up on us over time. It may be a gradual process of packing on pounds or slipping deeper and deeper into drinking, smoking, or using drugs. Maybe it's a matter of ignoring a worsening health problem, or a pattern of increasingly slacking off at work or spending more and more time away from the family.

We don't consciously choose to do these things, but they can and often do change our lives eventually just as if we had. At some point we realize that there's been a big change, sometimes for the worse. We have arrived at the point where our *roles, relationships, routines,* and *assumptions* have been altered.

On the other hand, some sleeper transitions can bring you—equally unaware—to a new place in your lives. Perhaps you've been growing and developing on the job, becoming more skilled and confident. You may be finding work less challenging but haven't given any thought to other career opportunities. Or perhaps you've become more worldly, interested in new foods, books, ideas, or friends, while your partner is stuck in a narrow sphere of interests and aspirations. Many people find it hard to imagine that over the years they have grown apart from someone they love.

At times, constructive and destructive sleeper transitions happen together. Frustration with a relationship or a job we have unwittingly outgrown may contribute to avoidance or to sliding into harmful habits as a way of coping. Being utterly absorbed in an avocation we love may lead us to ignore many other commitments, obligations, and relationships—even our health.

Sleeper transitions are tricky because we are usually in the midst of them before we recognize them. Even if you're growing, if you don't recognize the changes taking place and they're leaving you out of sync with your existing world, you can be in a very precarious position. By the time you realize how much you've changed, your behavior may already have kicked off a chain of events that precipitates an unexpected major transition. Jane is a case in point.

Jane's "The disquiet in my soul"

Jane wrote the following.

"The disquiet in my soul was triggered by my husband's long illness and my uncertainty about his health has gradually enlarged to the realities of aging.

"I have never been much for realities, preferring the sunshine of denial; this is particularly true in relation to chronology. I never thought I was too young for anything and never too old. But reality has reared its ugly head.

"As we trooped from doctor to doctor, I thought I'm not ready for 'old.' I find myself focusing on all those who have died or older friends who have moved to retirement communities, or friends who have various illnesses. One friend just had emergency quadruple bypass; two friends are facing hip replacements; two women in my office, in their early 50's, have cancer, and so it goes.

"Meanwhile I am having pain in my upper back and my foot, probably arthritis. I find I cannot do the gardening I once enjoyed; one of my colleagues asked if I was thinking of retiring.

"When did all this happen? But as I think how this crept up on me I remind myself that much of life is very good: beautiful blooming spring, concerts, lots of guests, eating, and being FAT."

Sleeper Dan

Here's the story of Dan, a friend who told me about his experience of waking up just in time to take advantage of a sleeper.

He was a much-valued technician in a biology laboratory, a man whose "magic" solutions for thorny technical problems had earned him the nickname "Dr. Fix-It." He enjoyed his work and his excellent reputation, but over the years Dan found himself increasingly absorbed in his weekend avocation, handcrafting stained glass. He had started by making little window hangings and had progressed to more ambitious and time-consuming projects such as elaborate decorations for Victorian doorways. He entered a few craft shows, sold a few pieces, and started to receive commissions, first from friends and then from strangers who had seen and admired his craftsmanship.

Dan found himself designing projects and sketching whenever he had a spare moment—even at his regular job. But one day as a result of a bad evaluation by his supervisor Dan realized that his heart was no longer in the lab, but in his home studio. With a wife and young son to support, Dan had never considered his stained-glass projects as more than a hobby. But the shock of the poor job evaluation made him look more carefully at how his time and energy were invested, and he realized that he would like to devote all his energy to working with the stained glass. To his surprise, when he shared his dreams with his wife, Bev, she was very supportive.

After taking a business course for artists and craftsmen, he saw that with careful planning, hard work, and a little luck, he might be able to shift careers and still make ends meet—barely. Together, Dan and Bev developed their "five-year plan": He would set up a formal business and try to establish himself as a professional craftsman while continuing in the lab. Bev would serve as his business manager and publicist. In a year or two, if the business seemed to be taking hold, he'd try to shift to doing the stained-glass work on a part-time basis, and a few years later, he would finally work on the stained glass full time. Once their son was a little older, Bev would return to work to help finance the business.

With this plan and goal in mind, Dan was able to keep his two work worlds separate. He went to his job in the lab with new energy and enthusiasm, and his work improved.

COUNTERTRANSITIONS: IT NEVER RAINS BUT IT POURS

Because our lives are often intertwined with other people's, our own lives may change when people close to us undergo major transitions. Mary's life had become a perfect example of what sociologist Gunhild Hagestad calls "countertransitions"—multiple transitions, many of which are connected to others in our lives.[2]

Although the case examples I've given on the preceding pages are drawn from real life, you may have noticed something unreal about them: for the most part, they sound as if people deal with a single transition at a time—even a single type of transition. But we all know it never seems to happen that way. Events and non-events never seem to come in single file. You might elect a transition, look forward to it—and then all of a sudden things begin to fall apart all around you: you're going to have a baby, and then your husband tells you he has just lost his job; you just moved in with a lover, and you discover that your mother, in failing health, wants to move in with you. Events in one area of your life trickle or tumble into other areas, and each one makes managing the others somewhat more difficult.

At times it feels as if the stars must be out of joint; surprises spring up, all unconnected, but all disruptive. At other times the transitions are part of a chain reaction in which one transition sets off a host of others. I call these pileups of related or unrelated transitions countertransitions.

Sometimes one event sets off a chain reaction, and your life feels like one crisis after another. Trouble erupts at every turn, for you and for everyone around you. Fortunately, for most people, these situations are fairly rare. Tough as these situations are to weather, most people manage to get through them. As the old saying goes, "When the going gets tough, the tough get going."

It doesn't take a string of catastrophes to add up to an overload of transitions. Even a run of good but disruptive transitions can bring on Excedrin headaches and more. Here are a few examples of the way some transitions can pile up at difficult times in our lives.

Unretiring Ben

The story of Ben, a man in his sixties, makes it clear that transitions often come in sets and can ricochet in unexpected directions. Ben began, well in advance, to make plans for his mandatory retirement from his company. He had no control over its timing, but because it was expected, he had time to prepare for it. He returned to graduate school to study accounting. As he said, "My strategy was to get into something new and leave the old completely behind. I resolved not to be a hang-around, not to keep going back to the old outfit."

Although older than many of the other students, Ben made friends easily and even started a support group for incoming students to the program. At first he was excited about preparing for a second career, but the school transition unexpectedly triggered some upsetting family transitions.

His wife, Ava, became increasingly critical of the fact that Ben was a student and no longer producing income. Somehow this unleashed mutual hostility that had been pent up for years. They decided to separate; but to save money, they lived separate lives in the same house until Ben received his degree and got a job. Later, Ben and Ava divorced, and not long afterward he remarried.

The multiple transitions in Ben's life seemed to start with just one—retirement. That prompted a return to school, followed by marital problems, eventually followed by a new job, a divorce, and remarriage. Ben's story illustrates the reality that transitions rarely happen singly. Rather, one elected transition can lead to an unexpected one, and then a whole train of other transitions may follow.

Martha—An Overwhelmed Writer

Martha, a freelance magazine writer, told me, "As for being overwhelmed . . . it's part of my personality to take on too much. And this past year and a half has been particularly difficult—lots of losses. My dad's twin brother and one of the homeless guys in my writing workshop both died. I was with him when he died. In addition, I broke off a five-year relationship and my friends were either adopting or having babies. Suddenly I felt completely alone. I kept the same job but it is isolating because I work at home. During this time I was also working on my advanced degree, and running the creative writing workshop at the shelter. I don't know if this happens to other people as well but everything always seems to happen to me at once. About seven or so years ago, I ended another long-term relationship, got sued, was in a car accident and had a melanoma removed." Martha sounded frantic as she described the pressures she felt.

Mary—Caught in the Middle

Mary, a middle-aged graduate student, is a study in transitions. Before she had a chance to grieve for the deaths of both her parents, her in-laws decided it was time to move to a retirement home. Because her husband, the breadwinner, couldn't afford to take leave from his job, she commuted out of town regularly to help his parents plan their move. At the same time, Mary's daughter, unable to afford her own apartment, moved back home; and her son and daughter-in-law had a baby just as he lost his job. To an outsider, Mary's situation was obviously overloaded with transitions. Yet, she was so unaware of the cumulative impact of these changes in her life that she could not understand why it was so hard to complete her graduate degree!

THE NATURE OF TRANSITIONS

Transition events and non-events that change our lives come in many sizes, types, and combinations. But it is not the actual event or non-event that overwhelms us. Remember, it is understanding how much these changes alter our lives—our *roles, relationships, routines,* and *assumptions.*

TYPES OF TRANSITIONS: A SUMMARY

Elected: Some are social milestones; others are individual choices

- Graduating from school
- Moving away from home
- Changing jobs
- Having a baby

- Retiring
- Moving
- Divorcing
- Becoming a grandparent

Surprises: When the unexpected happens

- Car accident
- Winning the lottery
- Death of a child
- Plant closing
- Getting a raise

Non-events: When the expected doesn't happen

- Infertility
- The promotion that doesn't occur
- The book that is never published
- The fatal illness that disappears
- The child who never leaves home

Life on Hold: The transition waiting to happen

- The long engagement
- Waiting to die
- Hoping to become pregnant
- Waiting for Mr. or Ms. Right

Sleeper Transitions: You don't know when they started

- Becoming fat or thin
- Gradually falling in love
- Becoming bored at work

Countertransitions: It never rains but it pours

- Retiring and losing a spouse
- Marrying, becoming a stepparent, and being promoted to a first supervisory job
- Having a baby, developing a serious illness, getting a new job
- Caring for ill children and parents at the same time

And many others

—⟨∞⟩—

IDENTIFY YOUR TRANSITION

Is it an event?

If so, is it an expected event?

Is it unexpected?

Is it a non-event?

Do you see your event or non-event as positive, negative, or neutral?

Has it, or will it, change your *roles*, *relationships*, *routines*, and *assumptions?*

Putting all this together, would you consider your transition event or non-event a BIG transition?

Do you feel overwhelmed?

If so, read on.

II

TAKING STOCK

Some of us breeze through what others may find a tragedy. Some feel panicked and lost even when their dream—a move to a new house, marriage to the perfect mate, landing the job they've always wanted—is suddenly coming true. We all have a combination of resources that we bring to each transition—what I call the 4 S System, your *Situation*, your *Self*, your *Supports*, and your *Strategies*. By TAKING STOCK of the 4 S's, as outlined in the following three chapters, you will build a foundation for understanding the nature of transitions and your own reactions to them.

We all approach every transition with potential resources for coping. It is important that we assess the state of these resources to see how well equipped we are to deal with the transition in question. For example, most people move a number of times in their lives. Sometimes they cope well; other times they manage with great difficulty. The reason: their resources—*Situation, Self, Supports*, and coping *Strategies*—differ with each move. TAKING STOCK of these four S's will give you a reading of your potential resources for managing a particular change.

PART II

We can understand the interplay of the 4 S's if we revisit the case of Melissa and Frank, whose move from their big house to a condo evoked concern. Eventually they adapted. First, they assessed their resources—their *Situation*, *Self*, *Supports*, and *Strategies*. They looked to see whether they could change these, change their meaning, reduce the pressures, or do nothing. Here's what they came up with. They could change the *Situation*. If life got unbearable in a condo, they could sell it and move back to another house.

Second, they examined their external resources, especially *Supports*, and realized that although their general supports were good, a negative support system was operating in the apartment. They decided to find at least two people with whom to develop a good relationship. As Melissa walked her dog and swam in the pool, she finally met two women who were delighted to have them as neighbors. Next they analyzed their inner strengths—their *Self* resource. They realized they needed to stop blaming themselves and start thinking differently about the *Situation*. Once they convinced themselves that the neighbors weren't right after all, their guilt reaction was replaced by assertiveness. When the next complaint came, Frank wrote back and said, "I refuse the complaint. Furthermore, I have a complaint to make—I feel we are being harassed." This example illustrates the interaction of *Situation*, *Self*, *Supports*, and *Strategies*.

3

TAKING STOCK
OF YOUR *SITUATION*

This chapter will guide you in assessing one of your four S's—your *Situation*. When you think back on all the transitions that you have made in your lifetime, you can probably remember some that you handled rather well and others that you handled less smoothly and with less satisfactory results. Since you are the same person, it may be puzzling that you could have pulled through one change like a trooper and yet floundered in the face of other, apparently less severe changes.

In chapter 2, I described different types of transition events and non-events, showing that some are anticipated and planned for, while others are unexpected and catch us by surprise. Some alter our lives dramatically; others do not. To understand your own *Situation*, it helps to identify your transition and try to attach one of those labels to it. But in order to take some of the mystery out of your transition, go beyond the label and ask yourself a series of questions: What are the characteristics of your particular *Situation* in terms of your planning for it, its timing in your life, your control of it, your previous experience with similar transitions, its permanence, and the presence of other stresses in your life?

Your answers to these questions will differ with each of your transitions. You will evaluate some as negative, others as positive, and many as a mixture. Some transitions will change your life in every regard; others in more limited ways. Some you will be able to plan for and control, but others will seem overwhelming and out of your control. Some will occur at a bad time in your life and add a burden to the stresses you already have, while others will add zest and sparkle to your life.

This chapter lists the factors that you must assess, consciously or unconsciously, when you TAKE STOCK of your *Situation*.

YOUR EVALUATION OF YOUR TRANSITION

You can evaluate your *Situation* by asking yourself these questions: Can you plan for it? Is it at a good time in your life? Can you control it? Is it fleeting or permanent? And how does it fit into the rest of your life? Psychologists Richard Lazarus and Susan Folkman found that individuals constantly ask: Is my transition good, bad, or neutral and do I have the resources for coping with the transition?[1]

They point out that the same apparent transition will be evaluated differently depending on the individual. For example, two young women have just delivered babies. One is thrilled. She and her husband have been trying to have a baby for several years. She is overwhelmed. This is a major transition that is changing every aspect of her life. But she is thrilled about it. The other young woman is a teenager, with very few resources. She is overwhelmed and evaluates the baby as negative. How will she care for it? What will she do about her own life?

Of course, one's evaluation can change. For example, one woman reported her anguish about a rift in her thirty-five-year-old friendship. By talking through the *Situation* with her therapist and reading books on women's friendships, she began to see that she was in the midst of a shifting relationship, not a final rift. She reevaluated her *Situation* from negative to okay. This modification enabled her to cope with the changing relationship.

Our evaluations are also colored by the way we view the world. Some of us are optimists and see the glass as half full, while others are pessimists who describe the same glass of water as half empty. Though a particular kind of change may seem only negative, it is impossible to make assumptions about how people will react to it. In the study of men whose jobs were eliminated at NASA's Goddard Space Flight Center, the late counseling psychologist Zandy Leibowitz and I found that most of the men felt "hit on the head" and "kicked in the back" when they first learned of the RIF (reduction in force).[2] They were terrified of the change, yet six months later typical reports from these men were "I feel like a king" and "I now know I can handle anything." They had been challenged by change. The week they learned about the job loss, all but two of the men we studied saw the change very negatively. A man who cut the grass reported, "I don't care about losing my job because I feel sure me and my buddies will get a job cutting grass someplace else." Similarly, a top executive saw opportunity rather than disaster. "This is great," he said. "I am so bored with my job, my wife, my life. This gives me the excuse I needed. I'm leaving everything and moving across country."

A famous line from Shakespeare's *Hamlet* is illuminating: "There is nothing either good or bad, but thinking makes it so." In other words, to one person a job loss can be the devastating last straw that destroys hope. But to another, it can present a challenge to take control and beat the illness down.

Your evaluation certainly affects your ability to cope. In a study of college students, for example, psychologists Christopher Peterson and Martin Seligman found that students' assessment of their own competence to handle exams was a better predictor of achievement than grade point average or SAT scores.[3]

You do not know anything about the nature of the transition for an individual until you know what it means to that person. The bottom line is this: You are more likely to embrace a change if you see it as one for the better or simply as neutral than if you see it as negative.

YOUR ABILITY TO PLAN

If you can anticipate a change, you can rehearse for it mentally, and often that makes the change easier. For three years, one woman rehearsed her departure from her husband. She knew exactly what she was going to do on the day that she left, so that when the time came, the inevitably painful transition was somewhat less anguishing.

Many middle-aged and older women begin rehearsing for widowhood. Since men die earlier than women and women traditionally marry older men, there is an expectation that women will live alone. This beginning preparation does not ease the pain but does act as a reality check about what to do next.

Marylu McEwen, Susan Komives, and I conducted a pilot study of men and women college presidents as they left their jobs. We learned that their ability to cope depended on whether or not leaving was voluntary and planned or involuntary and forced. Leave-taking is often difficult, but it is easier when you can plan and rehearse for it.[4]

There is some evidence that planning ahead for retirement can ease the pain of leaving your *roles*, *relationships*, *routines*, and *assumptions*. In fact, pre-retirement programs are cropping up as a way to push employees to think and plan about the future.

TIMING

The timing of a change is often as critical to your reaction as the type of change. Does the event come at a particularly difficult time in your life? Two men recovering from open heart surgery may have very different reactions to the operation and different levels of optimism about recuperation. One, for example, may be in physical pain, but may believe he is facing a bright future with a loving partner and a secure job. The other may have been abandoned by his wife, or his child may have been diagnosed with a severe illness, or he could be jobless. He will find it harder to dream of a better day.

Other examples with built-in timing problems include events such as a family move during the summer before a child's senior year of high school; a company layoff just before the employee's pension rights are vested; and the diagnosis of a serious illness in one partner of a couple about to marry. These unfortunately timed changes can double their normal impact, making it far more difficult for an individual to go through a change. Of course, a change can also occur when it is expected, or at an unexpected but ideal moment, making it much easier to cope. One forty-five-year-old woman had wanted to move to New York to work for many years. But she feared that because of her age and her relatively provincial background, no one would hire her. But with perfect timing, she was offered a fantastic job in New York just as her youngest child was going to college. In spite of her nerve-wracking adjustments to combine a serious career change and a dramatic move, she was able to face these more easily with her nest empty.

In analyzing a transition, it is also important to consider another kind of timing: the timing within the transition process itself.

As discussed in chapter 1, each transition is like a journey, with a beginning, a middle, and an end. At the beginning you think constantly of the change. The middle period is one of disruption, when you find yourself vulnerable: old norms and relationships are no longer relevant, and new ones are not yet in place. In the final period, you begin to fit the transition into the pattern of your life.

In many ways, the story of adult lives is the story of timing. When were you born—that is, during which historical period? Where are you in your family time? Are you proceeding according to what Bernice Neugarten labeled your "social clock?" This refers to the fact that people are always evaluating themselves in terms of whether or not they are "on time" or "off-time."[5] That is, are they engaging in behavior that seems appropriate? Appropriate behavior reflects our social, person-made clocks.

CONTROL OF THE TRANSITION

There are two kinds of control—the ability to influence life circumstances and, when that is not possible, the ability to control how one handles life circumstances. I used to say to my teenage son, "I cannot change the single-minded coach who expects you to play even with a concussion, but I can help you learn how to cope more effectively by considering the following possibilities: 1) you change the situation by getting off the football team; 2) you change the meaning of the situation by beginning to see football as just one activity and the coach's put-down of you as irrelevant; or 3) you cope by trying to relax, breathe deeply, and imagine yourself as you want to be on the field."

The ability to influence events, things, persons, and themselves gives people a sense of control. Psychologist Judith Rodin compared residents who were given some elements of control over their environment with others who were not. Not surprisingly, those given control over aspects of their lives lived longer than those given no control.[6]

I conducted a focus group with wives of football players. One of the wives echoed what others were feeling: "It just doesn't seem fair. For years I have been on hold while he has become a national hero. When will it be my turn? I feel as if my life is controlled by his schedule and needs, not mine." Another wife felt that both adults in a marriage or partnership should have equal control over who cooks, cleans, mends, and takes children to doctors and dentists; over who moves for a better job; over whose life "counts." She wondered, "Will that kind of equality ever exist for me?"

Divorce underscores the issue of control. If I were to interview the cast of characters involved in a particular divorce, I would find as many different stories about control as there are individuals. The couple's children, for example, might wish to prevent the divorce but realize that they are powerless to do so. The parents of the divorcing couple might also feel that they lack control. The couple who made the decision to divorce may feel in control of the decision, or one member of the couple may feel that it has been imposed while the other member who initiated it feels in control.

In divorce as in any other transition, people may use different methods to cope with the problem of feeling out of control. They may try to change the situation by negotiating, receiving mediation, cajoling, or even by legal means such as promoting legislation to protect grandparents' rights. Others might try to change the perceived meaning of divorce with comments like "This will really be better for the kids." Still others try to relax in the face of a difficult situation by jogging, meditating, or relaxing.

Transitions that are forced on us are far more difficult to manage than those we make by choice. In the study of men whose jobs were eliminated, one theme emerged: they were as concerned about their lack of *control* over the job loss as over the actual loss itself. One man told me, "This experience has been the most difficult in my life."

Family members may be affected in very different ways by a change in the job status of one person in the family. Psychiatrist Robert Seidenberg wrote about the trauma experienced by women who are asked to follow their successful husbands around the country as the husbands changed jobs. Such moves for a promotion demand very different coping strengths in a family.[7] The spouse who is being promoted has elected the change and is often excited and happy about the move. The spouse who follows feels forced into it by the need to keep the family together. This "follower" often feels depressed and unsettled, leaving friends, routine, and a familiar home. Children in such a family have different responses, depending on their *Situation*, *Support*, *Self*, and *Strategies*. Grandparents may feel very sad about "losing" an entire family. If invited to join the move, they might feel powerless. If not invited, they might feel deserted. We can, however, generalize that the more you feel you can control a *Situation*, the more likely you'll be able to manage it and to reduce the toll it takes on you.

PREVIOUS EXPERIENCE

Your previous experience can help you get through the transition facing you. Applying what you have learned can help you avoid becoming overwhelmed. Consider two people facing surgery. On the basis of previous experience, one patient may be able to focus on the anticipated surgery, rehearse for it, and prepare for it by recalling the factors that offered comfort and control during past surgeries. Another patient may feel terrified because of previous negative experiences. For this patient, the key might be to identify what made the previous experience negative—a dislike for a particular hospital or doctor, for instance—and try to determine how those factors can be avoided or ameliorated the second time.

Similarly, some families in the armed services or the Foreign Service say that they get used to resettling and even thrive on the experience by viewing the move in terms of the challenge of meeting new friends and becoming part of a new culture and lifestyle. Yet, for other families the stress of such moves can add up until finally someone says, "I've had it. Never again."

Previous experience is an important factor in coping, but only the individual involved can determine whether it is a plus or minus.

THE PERMANENCE OF THE TRANSITION

We regard a permanent change differently from one that we consider temporary. It is easier to endure—even a very painful transition—if we know that it won't last too long. For example, although no one looks forward to surgery, a brief stay in the hospital for a minor operation is easier to cope with than a diagnosis of a lifelong disability. A man may agree to move to another city so that his wife can enroll in a two-year training program, but only on condition that the move is temporary. He may need reassurance that they will return to their home community when her training is completed.

On the other hand, it feels good when something that is going well is seen as permanent. When interviewed by a television correspondent on *60 Minutes*, the new head of a major company said she loved her life at that moment—her family, her job, her money—and she wished that it could last forever.

THE REST OF YOUR LIFE

None of us leads a static life. Our lives are changing constantly, and the same transition may influence you differently under different circumstances. The other stresses in your life influence how you handle a particular transition. Consider the story of Julia, a clerical worker. She underwent a major transition in her life—her husband's job loss. When she described this event to me, it became clear that she and her family were overwhelmed. Her daughter Joan had been living with heart disease. Joan was president of her school class and an active skier and tennis player, and the family had to believe that the teenager's case was exceptional, that she would recover. Yet, at almost the same time that her father lost his job, Joan suffered a serious relapse and was hospitalized. This forced the family to face the prognosis that the youngster's life really was at stake. Earlier that year Julia's father had undergone eye surgery, and her mother-in-law had died. "I feel like a multiple-problem family," said Julia. The family felt stretched to its limits. Any one of these transitions—all undeniably negative—could reduce one's ability to cope. Bunched together, this set of changes all but incapacitated this family.

Some changes—even elected changes—can be disruptive. For many people, coping with multiple changes at once can cause stress. Whether you evaluate the changes as stressful or not, they do force you to use lots of strategies. To understand how an individual approaches and responds to a particular transition, it is necessary to look at the range of factors that add up to the context of the person's entire life.

SUMMARIZING YOUR *SITUATION*

As you think about making a change or weathering an existing one, you can ask yourself a series of questions about your *Situation*, your *Self* or inner strengths, your *Supports*, and your coping *Strategies*. In this chapter I focused on your *Situation*.

Is this *Situation* good or bad from your point of view? Is it positive or negative? Is it expected or unexpected? Does the transition come at the worst possible time or the best? Is it a move up or a move down? Where are you in the transition process—at the beginning, the middle, or the end?

When confronted with a transition, especially an unexpected or undesired one, it is easy for you to view your *Situation* as irrevocable or permanent. Yet, as we have seen in this chapter, analyzing a transition systematically shows that each one is different, that some are more significant than others, and that any irrevocability may be more deeply rooted in our own psychological makeup than in reality.

You can improve your ability to cope with transitions by learning how to measure the impact of a particular change: by placing it on a continuum of time and seriousness; by examining the effects it has had on your *roles*, *routines*, and *relationships;* and by becoming more aware of the effect of your own personality on how you view the situation.

Before going on to look at two other crucial S's—your *Self and* your *Supports*—you can analyze your *Situation* by filling out the chart titled "Your *Situation* Review."

YOUR *SITUATION* REVIEW

Were you able to

Plan for the transition in advance?	Yes	No
Control the transition?	Yes	No
Benefit from previous experience?	Yes	No

Was it a good time in your life?	Yes	No
Were there many other stresses in your life?	Yes	No

Did you evaluate your *Situation* as

Positive?	Yes	No
Negative?	Yes	No
Okay?	Yes	No

Taking everything into account, do you feel your *Situation* is

Okay?	Yes	No
Not okay?	Yes	No
A mixed bag?	Yes	No

4

TAKING STOCK
OF YOUR *SELF* AND
YOUR *SUPPORTS*

This chapter shows you how to take stock of your inner resource or your *Self* and the *Supports* that surround you.

YOUR *SELF*

We all bring many personal resources to our transitions. Some of these, like financial assets, are tangible. Others, like personality or outlook, are less obvious but just as important.

What do you bring of your *Self* to the many transitions you face? When you try to answer that question, you get into the interesting but challenging task of defining who you are. We have all heard people say, "You would really like Jane. She has a wonderful personality." What does that mean? Does it mean that Jane has traits that are considered "good" in our culture or group? Does it mean that Jane handles life with ease? Does it mean that she has a way of looking at things that makes her a pleasure to be with? These questions show that the process of understanding ourselves and what we bring to a transition is a complex one. Yet, we all know that a person's behavior and outlook are very critical to managing change.

Different Ways to Understand
An Individual's Inner Strengths

Since we cannot touch or see someone's inner resources, we will examine one individual, Steve, to illustrate how he TAKES STOCK of his inner resources.

Steve had a good income, enjoyed good health, and had many friends. He was married to his college sweetheart. He felt "on top of the world." But that world shattered when Steve and his vice president had a falling out over the direction the company should take. After a long political struggle, Steve was asked to resign. He felt crushed. At fifty-eight, he felt too old to go looking for another job and too young not to work. Soon after, his wife died of a heart attack. Steve had to face two potentially devastating transitions, which exaggerated his fears of aging and loneliness. Over time, he found a job in a nonprofit organization. He met new people and developed some very close relationships. Many of Steve's friends attribute his eventual triumph to his inner strengths and resources.

Some would say that Steve has a "hardy personality"; others would point to Steve's wisdom, perspective, and humor; many might point to his resilience and flexibility, which are invaluable in enabling someone to bounce back and change course.

Resilience is clearly a dominant theme in psychological literature. George Vaillant wrote, "Resilience reflects individuals who metaphorically resemble a twig with a fresh, green living core. When twisted out of shape, such a twig bends, but it does not break; instead, it springs back and continues growing."[1] Steve bent but did not break.

Psychologist Salvatore Maddi studies the relationship between resilience and hardiness. He wrote, "There are multiple pathways to resilience under stress . . . and . . . hardiness" is one.[2] Specifically, hardiness is an attitude that "helps in transforming stressors from potential disasters into growth opportunities," thereby promoting resiliency. According to Maddi, a hardy individual is someone who exhibits certain attitudes or approaches to life. First, the individual is involved and committed, feels in control of outcomes, and is challenged by negative occurrences. By contrast, a person who distances from others, feels passive in the face of challenges, and avoids facing the issue does not exhibit hardy behavior and therefore will be less resilient.

Maddi and his team studied the Illinois Bell Telephone (IBT) company over a period of ten years after the workforce had been dramatically and drastically reduced. Some of the managers crumbled under the stress while others embraced it and moved on. The latter showed commitment, control, and challenge.

Psychologist Shelley Taylor identified five different ways people responded to a diagnosis of breast cancer.[3] "Fighting-spirits"—those with the will to fight, struggle, and resist—and "deniers"—those who refused to recognize the reality of the situation—had less recurrence of the disease. The other three types—the "stoics," who submitted without complaint to unavoidable life circumstances; the "helpless persons," who felt unable to cope without the help of others; and the "magical thinkers," who believed that help would come through mysterious and unexplained powers—all had higher recurrence rates.

Another way to take stock of your *Self* and your inner resources is by identifying the degree to which you feel good about yourself— what psychologists Grace Baruch and Rosalind Barnett and writer Caryl Rivers have called a sense of "well-being."[4] They studied three hundred women to determine the factors contributing to well-being. Some of the women they studied had never married, others were married without children, some were married with children, and others were divorced with children. The authors found that those who put energy into several areas of their lives, such as work and family, were more satisfied than those who put all their eggs into only one basket, such as work or family. The authors concluded that investing in several aspects of life leads to a combination of mastery, pleasure, and a sense of well-being.

In the case of Steve, we can assume that he was overwhelmed at first because his sense of well-being had been totally disrupted. His balance of mastery and pleasure was shaken. But because of who he is, Steve was able to take on this challenge and once again gain control and balance in his personal and work life.

Many in transition feel helpless. A partner leaves you, your plant closes, birthdays keep accumulating, you choose to move to a new city. Many people experience these events as overwhelming. Are you the kind of person who usually gives up? Or do you meet the challenge head-on and try to take control?

We have discussed how Martin Seligman's work focused on different ways people react, especially to negative, uncontrollable, or bad events. According to Seligman, those who feel they have control over their lives, or who feel optimistic about their own power to control at least some portions of their lives, tend to experience less depression and achieve more at school or work; they are even in better health. Seligman suggested that the individual's "explanatory style"—the way a person thinks about the event or transition—can explain how some people weather transitions without becoming depressed or giving up. Since many transitions are neither "bad" nor "good" but a mixture, a person's "explanatory style" becomes the critical key to coping. A person with a positive explanatory style is an optimist, while one with a negative style is basically a pessimist.[5]

For example, we can ask how Steve explained what happened to him. Did he blame himself and say he lost out on the job because he was inadequate? Did he conclude that he would always be inadequate at work? People who blame themselves for everything that happens and then generalize to think they always "screw things up" have a good chance of being depressed and passive. On the other hand, Steve saw that he clearly had some role in the job decision and that, in general, he handles complex situations well; he thus had a good chance of coming out on top in a transitional situation.

Steve's success in managing and weathering his transition suggests that he is probably an optimist and that his "explanatory style" is positive. Peterson and Seligman suggested that a person's explanatory style can predict success on a job. In a study of insurance salespersons, those representatives with a "positive explanatory style" were twice as likely as those with a "negative style" to still be on the job after a year. Following up on this study, a special force of a hundred representatives who had failed the insurance industry test but who had a "positive explanatory style" were hired. They were much more successful than the pessimists.[6]

Another way to TAKE STOCK of personal resources is to use personality tests such as the Myers-Briggs Type Indicator. This test, developed by Isabel Myers and Kathryn Briggs, is based on Jung's descriptions of different "personality types." This easy-to-score, easy-to-take personality test gives people an indication of how they habitually view life and its problems and shows how they make decisions about how to handle them.[7]

Some of us navigate through life by using intuition, and others navigate by using senses, like eyes and ears, to uncover the facts in a realistic way. Some people make decisions in a logical, systematic way; others do so by feeling what seems right. People can be differentiated along these dimensions. It may be helpful for you to try to determine how you and your family or acquaintances tend to function based on these criteria. Recognizing that your type might be different from that of your partner, boss, or friend may help you understand, for example, why you work well with one colleague and conflict with another. It could be a simple matter of different ways of understanding and approaching the world. Acknowledging these differences can be helpful in building collaboration rather than conflict.

I have used words like *stress*, *transition*, and *coping*. These words are used by psychologists in many different ways. Some define *stress* as an outside stimulus; others define it as a response to a stimulus. Others, like Lazarus and Folkman, define *stress* as a "particular relationship between the person and the environment that is appraised by the person as taxing or exceeding his or her resources and endangering his or her well-being."[8] Others who face major transitions—those that change many *roles*, *routines*, *relationships*, and *assumptions*—as Steve did may be challenged by them. Steve, who faced a very stressful set of transitions, was nevertheless challenged rather than overwhelmed. It is the interaction of the *Situation* and one's *Self* that explains reactions to transition.

Regardless of whether these are innate or learned qualities, it is my conviction that all of us can increase the number of our coping strategies, thereby becoming more flexible and resilient. As we will see in chapter 5, the person who uses many strategies flexibly is the one who masters change. I believe we can learn how to increase our coping repertoire and build on what we already have.

To summarize: To TAKE STOCK of your *Self* and your inner resources, you can ask yourself some questions:

- Are you challenged or overwhelmed by transition events or non-events? Which kinds of "stress" challenge you? Overwhelm you?
- Do you approach transitions as a fighting spirit, a stoic, a denier, a helpless person, or a believer in magic?
- Do you feel a sense of control or mastery as you face transitions? Do you usually balance mastery and pleasure?
- Do you face life as an optimist or a pessimist?

YOUR *SUPPORTS*

Steve, who had lost both his job and his wife in a short period of time, needed a great deal of support despite his optimism and resilience. His friends were sympathetic and made the appropriate number of visits and phone calls. But they did not realize that the loss of support and intimacy, coupled with his fear of diminishing options because of his sex and age, made him feel that he had lost everything that had given meaning to his life.

Steve did not want to burden his friends, but he also knew he needed some extra support. Being creative, he visited his local church and joined a group called "Out of Work: Working it Out." He built in a temporary support system without unduly burdening his friends.

Pat's transition began when her good friend had a stroke at the age of forty. Pat thought, "If my friend is incapacitated, it could happen to me or my husband. If something happened to my husband, I am not prepared to support my family of six children." Around the same time, Pat's interest was piqued by a newspaper ad for a women's external degree program. Since the program required only occasional weekends on campus, she began to think that it might be possible for her to complete the degree she had begun years ago and to prepare herself to be self-supporting. Pat's husband, Bob, was very supportive when they initially discussed the idea of her returning to school. But when Pat was gone for three days at a time every six weeks Bob complained and even ridiculed her. Pat was so determined to complete the degree that she asked her mother to move in during the times she was away. The support of her mother and of the program made up for her husband's negative behavior.

We see that even when people are in fairly stable relationships, we cannot assume a totally supportive situation. In interviews about support, I now ask, "In what ways is X supportive of you or your activities? In what ways could X be more supportive?" It seems that support is often a double-edged sword. In many instances support is given in exchange for some measure of control. The unwritten statement is "I'll support you, but you need to behave as I think you should."

Some people give support but in a way that is not helpful. One woman wrote, "My boyfriend of five years told me he was one step away from being in love with another woman. This called into question my past assumptions about our relationship. I began to doubt myself." When I asked what helped her cope, she said, "professional counseling." When asked if she had tried methods that were unhelpful, she replied, "Simply talking with friends. They could not understand—they were too biased. Their reactions ranged from pity for me to total anger. Although my friends meant well, they were ineffective." This is a case where friends did not give the kind of support she needed.

Support is a very general concept. As a way to get a handle on it, I will describe what it is, where it comes from, and then show you how to visualize your own *Support* as you move through, tackle, face, or master your transitions.

Support—What It Is

We all have a visceral sense of what the word *support* means, of what we seek from friends, relatives, church, neighbors, coworkers, or even strangers. But understanding the functions of support—why it is important to us—is a bit more complicated.

Support systems help individuals mobilize their resources by sharing "tasks," providing "extra supplies of money, materials, tools, skills," and giving guidance about ways to improve coping. Psychologists Robert Kahn and Toni Antonucci identified the following functions of support:[9]

- *Affection*—an expression that someone respects, likes, or loves you;
- *Affirmation*—an expression that someone agrees that what you have done is appropriate or understandable;
- *Assistance* or *aid*—an expression that someone will actually supply you with chicken soup, information, time, or whatever tangible help is necessary to get you over the crisis.

Where It Comes From

People receive affection, affirmation, and aid in many ways, from many sources. Sometimes they receive support from friends, but in other instances it comes from a professional. People can potentially get support from many sources: intimates, families, friends, strangers, and institutions. You, the person in transition, need to evaluate what kind of support you need—affection, affirmation, aid—and from what source you could receive it—friend, partner, stranger, or institution. Do you need support from one constant source, or would it help to have the comfort of a group of people who face similar problems? Today many people join self-help groups where they both give and receive support.

Intimates

We often extol the virtues of an intimate relationship, but sometimes the person with whom we are most intimate cannot be our best support. The men whose jobs were eliminated, for example, resisted going to their wives, mostly because they felt guilty about inflicting this transition on their families. In one extreme case, a man actually dressed and pretended to go to work. His wife didn't discover this until the unemployment checks began to arrive.

Despite these examples, most research confirms the importance of having an intimate—someone with whom you can share honestly and openly your inner world. Intimates are extremely important during transitions. Intimate support comes in several packages: the intimacy you can achieve with friends who are often part of your adult life; the intimacy you can achieve with your spouse or partner; and the more permanent intimacy you receive from parents, siblings, and children.

Family

Family can be a key source for giving and receiving affection, affirmation, assistance—and, at times, honest feedback. In most of our lives, the "forever" relationships are intergenerational, between grandparents, parents, and children. Without wanting to glorify these relationships (because they, like all others, are fraught with ambivalence and stress as well as support), we realize that they are central to our feelings of well-being. As we live longer, an increasing number of us continue to be part of four- or five-generation families. Sociologist Gunhild Hagestad, a demographer and researcher specializing in families and aging, observed, "These family patterns, unprecedented in human history, have in a way taken our society by surprise. . . . Families today may have to sort out who gives help and support to whom when two generations face aging problems."[10] One woman about to retire felt obligated to have her mother move in with her when her mother became ill and depressed. The daughter was not happy about the prospect of spending her retirement years with her mother, since there had always been friction between them. But she realized that although she might be aggravated, she wasn't lonely. Most studies show that adult children stay in touch with their aging parents and that family members constitute the greatest sources of assistance to one another.

Friends

Support from friends, lovers, and partners also helps buffer stress, but the type of support they provide may differ from that provided by the family. Lillian Rubin found in her study of friendships that "friends help in the lifelong process of self-development, often becoming . . . people who join us in the journey toward maturity, who facilitate our separation from the family and encourage our developing individuality."

Thus, she points out, "One of the most valued gifts friends offer us [is]—a reflection of the self we most want to be. In the family it's different. There, it's our former selves that are entrenched in both the family's vision and our own." Rubin points to the changing functions and roles of friends and asserts that it is important to have a number of different types of intimates. She had found from countless interviews that "even when people are comfortably and happily married, the absence of friends exacts a heavy cost in loneliness and isolation."[11]

Strangers

When Rodney, a community organizer, found he had cancer, he fought it with all the energy he could muster. He went to the best doctors and even became part of a research experiment, but he went through physical and mental agony. His wife and adult children were totally supportive, and he also benefited from the support of a set of very close friends who had known the family since college days.

At the time of his diagnosis, Rodney was negotiating a major grant from a foundation. When the foundation learned that he had cancer, the negotiations fell apart. The feeling that he would now have to face a financial crisis on top of a life-threatening disease devastated Rodney. He explained the situation to his doctor, a relative stranger, who wrote a letter to the foundation explaining the circumstances of Rodney's disease and suggesting that the foundation would be guilty of discrimination if it did not provide the funds. As a result of the letter, the foundation's decision was reversed and Rodney received the grant. This case illustrates the necessity of having access to a variety of types of support—support from intimates, from friends, and from strangers.

A professional woman who lives in Washington, DC, went to Denver to make a speech. When she arrived at the hotel where the meeting was scheduled, she learned that she arrived one month early. Unable to comprehend that she had done this, she was momentarily very upset. To compensate, she decided to treat herself to a lovely lunch at one of the best restaurants in town. The maitre d' was friendly, and the woman found herself telling him about her terrible error. He laughed and told her about a mistake he had made. This interchange with a stranger was enormously helpful, and by the time lunch was over, she had regained her humor and perspective.

Institutions and Organizations

One woman described how she coped with widowhood: "The transition was unanticipated and outside my control, so there was a high degree of stress. This was balanced by an environment of tremendous social support from family, friends, and my department at work. I could not have survived without the constant telephone calls, concern, and continuous offers of help. I was surprised at my initiative in creating a support group of single women to share common concerns."

Many people do not have the energy to create a new ad hoc support group. Fortunately, many existing organizations are already available to support us in times of change. There are many single-purpose organizations such as Alcoholics Anonymous (AA), where alcoholics offer advice and strength to others. The idea behind AA has been expanded to other special-purpose organizations, such as Gamblers Anonymous, Overeaters Anonymous, and many more such groups.

Other single-purpose groups have sprung up. These include Parents Without Partners, caregivers of those with Alzheimer's disease, and parents of disabled children, including those with learning disabilities, mental illness, and physical illness.

More general are institutions such as Family Services, Red Cross, Travelers Aid, and the various social welfare and counseling arms of religious, ethnic, and national groups.

Then, of course, there are a host of organizations created to deal with special groups: women, Hispanics, blacks, immigrants, the foreign-born, homosexuals, and other groups that have not been getting their share of support from society.

In addition, there are organizations such as unions, professional business, trade groups, and churches that offer formal services in addition to the tremendous resource of the "people power" of fellow congregants, who can and do become helpers at least and friends at best.

Whether you are facing a troubling situation or initiating a desired change, the support you receive from institutions can be invaluable.

Different Supports for Men and Women

The support networks and intimate relationships available to us depend on many factors—where we live, our age, our economic status, our own personality. But some research suggests that sex is a particularly important determinant of the composition of one's support. Men and women live in somewhat different worlds—one major difference stems from the changing sex ratio over the course of life. Although more boys are born than girls, by the time people are in their mid-thirties, there are more women than men. This imbalance has resulted in remarriage becoming a disproportionately male experience after age forty. By the time people are in their eighties, there are more than twice as many women as men. Thus, the majority of older women are widowed and have a social life with other women, while most older men are married and have a social life with couples.

A landmark UCLA study found that women respond differently to stress than men. Furthermore, their bonds with other women are long lasting and serve as buffers to stress. Friends clearly help people live longer by lowering blood pressure, heart rate, even cholesterol. Women are the ones that connect and maintain relationships with other women, making women's friendships special.[12]

The types of *Supports* we need and can offer may change depending on our age and circumstances. The demographics of age and sex may impinge on our ability to get the type of *Supports* we need at the time we need them. Hagestad's interviews with grandparents, middle-aged men, and women and their adult children suggest that men's ups and downs are tied more often to the world of work and politics, while women's are related more to events in the family. Furthermore, she found that when men get together, they talk about work, education, money, and social issues, while women focus more on interpersonal relations and family.[13]

Support for the Supporter

Often we forget that a person who is giving support to a friend or family member may also require some support to help shoulder the additional burden. We can see this in the case of Mark, whose sister Sarah confided that she was having her second abortion and swore him to secrecy. Mark became Sarah's rock through the trauma, although it was extremely difficult for him since his political and philosophical views about the morality of abortion were in flux at the time of Sarah's confidence. Because Mark loved Sarah, he stuck by her and didn't tell her about his own changing views. In addition, he couldn't confide in any of his friends about the stress of being Sarah's supporter because this was Sarah's secret. Mark was helping Sarah to cope, but he needed support so that he could continue being her supporter.

Another example is Adele, a woman whose best friend's baby died. Adele's role was coordinating the funeral and friends' visits. She reported that she had no time to mourn the loss herself and felt stressed by her coordinating role. She, too, felt a need for tender loving care.

Because life is by definition a series of transitions for all of us, the specific individuals with whom we have supportive relationships change as life unfolds, and the options for relationships also change. We also require different *types* of support at different times.

A Way to Visualize the Range of Your Supports

Kahn and Antonucci have developed a way for you to identify your potential *Supports* by drawing a series of concentric circles with you

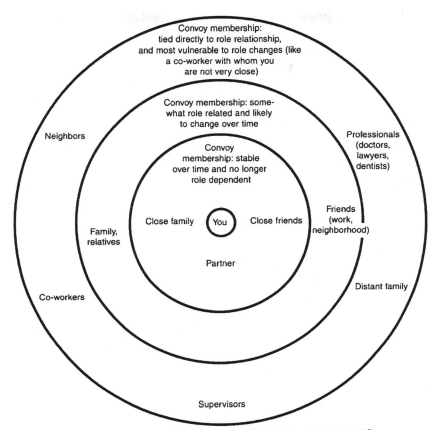

FIGURE 4.1.   YOUR "CONVOY OF SOCIAL SUPPORT"
Source: Based on work from R. L. Kahn and T. C. Antonucci, "Convoys over the Life Course: Attachment, Roles, and Social Support," in *Life-Span Development and Behavior,* edited by P. B. Baltes and O. C. Brim, Jr. (New York: Academic Press, 1980), 273. Reprinted by permission.

at the center (see figure 4–1). The circle closest to you contains your closest, most intimate friends and family, who are presumably part of your life forever. The next circle is for family, friends, and neighbors who are important in your life but not in the intimate way the first group is. The circle farthest away from you represents institutional supports. Kahn and Antonucci call these circles an individual's "convoy of social support," which are carried through life.[14]

Transitions shift one's supports. By mapping out your *Supports* in concentric circles you can visualize how your transition alters your support system. For example, geographical moves can interrupt relationships between husbands and wives. Spouses who do not want to move but do so for the sake of the family may harbor deep resentment and anger. Thus, a wife who follows her husband may have had him in the center of her life before the move, but she may shift him to one of the more distant circles after it. In a contrasting case, a new college administrator reported that his wife was delighted with their move back to Washington, DC, because she lived there when she was younger and therefore has a large support network. If we were to compare her concentric circles before and after the move, her husband's place would be the same—in the closest circle.

Other examples can be readily found by looking at what happens to people's support systems before and after retirement. If a newly retired couple moves away from many *Supports* to a place with none, the transition may be very difficult. If, however, retirement liberates one of the spouses to move back to an area where there are intimate relatives and friends, then it might be a much easier transition. This system of concentric circles shows that the most important aspect of a transition may not be the change itself but what it does to the individual's "convoy."

To take stock of your *Supports* you can ask yourself:

- Am I getting what I need for this transition in terms of affection? Affirmation? Aid?
- Do I have a range of types of *Support*—spouse or partner, other close family or friends, coworkers/colleagues/neighbors, organizations, strangers, and institutions?
- Has my *Support* system or "convoy of social support" been interrupted by this transition?
- Do I feel my *Support* system for this transition is a low or a high resource?

PUTTING IT TOGETHER: THE CASE OF DAVID

David, a top administrator in the state highway patrol, returned to school to earn a degree that would enable him to become a teacher when he retired. Full of enthusiasm, he enrolled in a state university. To all appearances David was a responsible, dedicated professional who had identified teaching as a means of making the transition to a second career in his retirement years. Yet, two years and a lot of hard work later, he dropped out of school without finishing the requirements for the degree. "I feel disappointment, some resentment, and at times anger," he said after the experience. "I usually achieve what I start out to achieve."

What went wrong? David thought he had accumulated enough credits to graduate by taking courses at the university and by enrolling in a program designed to evaluate prior experience and, if appropriate, award credit. The process of applying for such credit is complicated and requires the learner to develop a detailed portfolio of each experience. David applied for his B.A. degree, only to discover that although he had enough credits, many were from community college courses, and he did not have enough from the university. When he realized that he still needed sixty more credits that had to be taken on the campus, David became infuriated and dropped out of school.

In order to understand what happened, let's TAKE STOCK of David's *Situation*, *Self*, and *Supports*. In the next chapter we can TAKE STOCK of his *Strategies*.

TAKING STOCK of David's Situation

There were many pluses in David's *Situation*. The transition was one he had elected, and he was beginning to see himself as someone who could make his career dreams come true. However, his *Situation* had some negatives. For example, his changed *routines* required that he drive ninety miles each way twice a week. He had to plan carefully so that, in addition to the drive, he could find time to study as well as work and spend quality time with his family. David felt that his family was getting the short end of the stick. But, despite the negatives, he was pleased about the transition to learner and evaluated it positively.

TAKING STOCK of David's Self

David described himself as a "hard worker," a "go-getter." He classified himself as a "fighting spirit" and an "optimist," but he added, "If things don't go the way I think they should, I can fly off the handle. Maybe I am a little short on patience." So David may be his own best and worst resource. He fights for what he wants and believes in, but he may give up if the odds seem unfavorable.

TAKING STOCK of David's Supports

David assessed his family support as "terrific." His wife took on additional family responsibilities so that he could give his all to getting his degree. He also felt positively about his coworkers' support. Some teased him about going to school, but mostly they thought it was great. He was getting a good supply of affection, affirmation, and aid.

David's downfall was his perceived lack of institutional support. He claimed he never received information about the credit limitations from outside institutions. The dean claimed that David was informed but was so eager that he didn't pay attention to advice to slow down. Whatever the facts, there was clearly a breakdown in communication—a breakdown that prompted David to leave.

When we TAKE STOCK of his *Situation*, *Self*, and *Supports* two crucial insights emerge:

- *Self* and many *Supports* offer both positives and negatives in terms of a strong sense of our preparation for and ability to deal with a transition

- What determines our success is *how we evaluate* the transition and our resources for coping with it.

YOUR *SELF* REVIEW

• Are you challenged rather than overwhelmed by transitions?	Yes	No
• Do you feel a sense of control or mastery as you face transitions?	Yes	No
• Do you usually face life as an optimist rather than as a pessimist?	Yes	No
• Do you define yourself as resilient in the face of change?	Yes	No
• Taking all of the above into account, do you rate your *Self as*:		
Okay?	Yes	No
Not okay?	Yes	No
A mixed bag?	Yes	No

YOUR *SUPPORT* REVIEW

• Are you getting what you need for this transition in terms of:		
Affection?	Yes	No
Affirmation?	Yes	No
Aid?	Yes	No
• Do you have a range of types of support: spouse or partner, other close family or friends, coworkers/colleagues/neighbors, organizations, strangers?	Yes	No

- Have you checked the institutions that are available to you? Yes No
- Has your "convoy of social support," from intimate to institution, been interrupted by this transition? Yes No
- Do you regard your *Support* for this transition as:
  Okay? Yes No
  Not okay? Yes No
  A mixed bag? Yes No

5

TAKING STOCK
OF YOUR *STRATEGIES*

It's easy to identify things that upset you; what's hard is deciding what to do about your feelings and the situations that give rise to them. Confronting very challenging transitions often makes us feel helpless and therefore hopeless. We may feel that we have little control over our *Situation* and that our options are few. But in fact there are more *Strategies* and options than we realize. You already have a repertoire of coping *Strategies* that have helped you in the past. But when the going gets tough, you may well need to expand them further.

To help you TAKE STOCK of your coping repertoire, I will present two ways of organizing coping strategies drawn from the work of experts who study coping and from the wisdom and experience of friends, students, and people I have interviewed and counseled.

Sociologists Leonard Pearlin and Carmi Schooler interviewed 2,300 people between the ages of eighteen and sixty-five living in the Chicago area in order to identify the major coping strategies people used as they faced life's strains and joys.[1] They distinguished three types of coping strategies: those that *change the situation*, those that *change its meaning*, and those that *help you relax*. I added a fourth; knowing when to *do nothing* or *take deliberate inaction*.

Having a variety of coping strategies in mind can help you expand and diversify your coping repertoire; it helps you identify those you already use and suggests new ones to try. Pearlin tells us that there is no single magic-bullet coping strategy. The effective coper is someone who can use many *Strategies* flexibly, depending on the *Situation*.

Geraldine, a graduate student, demonstrated the usefulness of Pearlin and Schooler's work. She said, "When confronted with learning difficulties, I used strategies to *change the situation* by seeking tutoring help. I also negotiated with teachers to allow me to do things in my own way. For example, I was terrified of giving an oral report in class. My teacher said I could do it at home into a tape recorder and then bring the tape to class.

"Second, I tried to *change the meaning* by redefining my disability and seeing it as a way to help others by becoming an advocate for others challenged as I had been. I often say, 'Who cares if I don't know east from west, read slowly, and write backwards?'

"Third, I try to *relax* by playing lots of racquetball, often screaming to let off steam. I am part of an extremely strong and caring support group, and I'm proficient at networking to find individuals who can assist me."

When faced with a challenge we can ask ourselves, Can I change the *Situation?* If not, can I change the meaning of the *Situation?* And can I employ some *Strategies* to help me relax? Asking these three questions serves as your guide for how to proceed. Remember, however, that there are times when it is best to sit and wait. For example, Warren the caregiver, briefly described in chapter 1, was urged by many health care workers to take action by placing his mother and sister in institutional settings. He resisted. "I am glad I did nothing about that. For me, it is right to be a caregiver and keep them at home."

Psychologists Richard Lazarus and Susan Folkman organize coping effectiveness in a slightly different way. These psychologists focus on the individual's "cognitive appraisal." Very simply, this means that every time an individual faces a challenge, the individual appraises it: Is it benign? Is it a threat? Is it positive?[2] Clearly, Geraldine saw her learning disability as a threat to her competency and self-esteem. As you evaluate your transition, you will also engage in a second kind of appraisal: Do I have the resources to cope with the challenge? When you are totally overwhelmed, as Warren was with caring for his mother and sister, you often cannot think what to do. If you use Lazarus and Folkman's method, you can ask yourself, What can I do about the challenge? If there is hope, they suggest using "problem-focused" strategies. If hope is absent, then they suggest using "emotion-focused strategies." There is clearly an overlap between these two models of coping.

Geraldine used both. She was constantly problem solving. For example, she became a reading specialist so she could first help herself and now can help many others by serving as an advocate for learning-disabled children. Geraldine used "emotion-focused" strategies by making positive comparisons. She wrote, "When I received my Graduate Record Examination scores I was devastated by the mundane results. I was overwhelmed by a feeling of stupidity. Then I thought about some of the bizarre things that have happened and I said to myself: 'Damn, but look how far you have come!'"

Geraldine is a master of diverse coping strategies, and that mastery has paid off handsomely in helping her achieve despite her disability. You can expand your own repertoire by using some of the strategies described here. I have organized these strategies to conform to Pearlin and Schooler's model: *Strategies* to change the situation, to change the meaning of the transition, or to reduce one's stress.

STRATEGIES TO CHANGE OR MODIFY THE TRANSITION

All of us confront situations that we want to change. The concept of options includes elements of desire and hope that there is an alternative route. Seeing, creating, and using options are crucial to passing through life's transitions successfully. One factor that can transform a transition into a crisis is the inability to see any options for escaping from a bad situation.

We can search for external options, which are opportunities that exist in a tangible sense: a job, a school, a person who will help you. For example, Ann lived in a small town and worked for the telephone company. The option of attending college was unavailable until the phone company and a university offered extension classes in her town for telephone employees. Ann explained her use of options this way. She had the dream of attending college, but because she lived in a rural community she had no access to a college. As soon as extension courses were available to her, she enrolled. She exercised choice when there was an external opportunity to do so.

In addition, there are less tangible options that depend on your perceptions. For example, when Ivan Charner and I studied clerical workers, we asked, "Generally, in change situations how do you perceive options?" Ninety-four percent said that they saw more than one option. However, when we asked, "For the transition you selected as one that really changed your life this past year, how many options did you perceive?" over 34 percent said they saw only one. These responses provided an important insight. People in the midst of a transition often freeze and can see only one option.[3]

Jim, a stockbroker, lived a double life: life in the outdoors, roughing it; and the life he lived in business suits and fancy offices. He had seen no way to reconcile these two lifestyles. Finally, he broke out of his it-can't-be-done mode. He convinced his company to let him open an office in Montana. He goes to work in boots, lives an outdoor life, and keeps in touch with clients by e-mail, fax, and phone. He could have spent his whole life not living out the dream. Instead he created options.

This all sounds easy, but we know that the process of generating and perceiving options can be difficult. How can we make it happen? The triggering process is often not a conscious one. A business executive named Mort was prompted unexpectedly into creating options for himself. After retiring from the business he founded, Mort found that his colleagues no longer sought his company for lunch. Miserable and depressed, he could see no way to overcome this negative side of retirement. Then Mort received a phone call from an executive with another company asking him to address participants in a pre-retirement seminar. This turned the tide. As he prepared the speech, Mort began to see new possibilities for his own life, helping employees and companies with the transition from work to retirement. He wrote a book on the subject that created a new life and career for himself, in which he lectured on the topic all over the country.

These examples provide a lesson: There is no single magic way to get the ball rolling. For some people in transition, options suddenly become evident because they read something in a book or newspaper; they talk to a friend; or they have a confrontation. The critical ingredients are to remain committed to the importance of the search and to "hang in there" for as long as it takes.

You probably have some typical ways of trying to alter things. Maybe it's through negotiating or taking direct action. But there are other strategies, too, including seeking advice, asserting yourself, brainstorming to develop an alternative plan, or even taking legal action when needed. Have you used all of these?

Negotiating

You can sometimes turn a no-win situation into a winning one by negotiating: sit down, talk things through, and see the other person's point of view and assumptions. We are always negotiating, but some people are better at it than others, and some people learn how to improve their negotiating skills through training. People can learn and apply such skills in many areas, including labor-management relations, supervisor-supervisee relations, couple relationships, and parent-child relationships.

Gerard I. Nierenberg, president of the Negotiation Institute, defined the potential of negotiation:

> Nothing could be simpler in definition or broader in scope than negotiation. Every desire that demands satisfaction—and every need to be met—is at least potentially an occasion for people to initiate the negotiating process. Whenever people exchange ideas with the intention of changing relationships, whenever they confer for agreement, they are negotiating.[4]

Stephanie's story illustrates the importance of negotiating in changing a situation. She wrote:

> My transitions relate to my eye problems. I had severe and pervasive eye hemorrhages. My already poor vision was almost lost entirely for two months. I was helped to cope by several things. First, when I realized that I was becoming legally blind, I went to a career counselor. As a result of that, I began taking courses so I could shift to a type of work that made fewer demands on my eyesight.
>
> Second, when this latest incident occurred, I called my boss and began negotiating a way to change my work assignment. I explained my needs and recognized his. To meet his needs, I tried to figure out the parts of the job I could do without top vision.

Taking Optimistic Action

There are times when people are in a situation they define as negative, but instead of wallowing in it, they take some action to solve the problem and try to find a solution. They stick to it, never giving in to those tempting feelings of helplessness. That's optimistic action.

Some families with chronically ill children use this strategy frequently. They constantly seek out new information on the illness and try to keep their home situation and their child's life as normal as possible. Taking action keeps the family mobilized.

Learning Resilience

As pointed out in chapter 4, it is better for one's mental health to be resilient and exhibit characteristics of hardiness. But what if you are not resilient? Can you learn to be? On the American Psychological Association's (APA) website, *Psychology Matters*,[5] there is a report of Dr. Salvatore R. Maddi and Deborah M. Khoshaba's training program. They train people how to turn stressors into opportunities by "situational reconstruction," so that they begin to imagine "alternative ways of thinking about the stressor."[6] The team developed workbooks that take the participant step by step through a process of looking at adversity, dealing with it, and even growing from it by staying involved, not giving up, remaining calm, and making a plan.

The APA initiated a program to help children, teenagers, and adults adapt well to adversity, trauma, tragedy, threats, and other significant sources of stress. In the fall of 2003, the APA launched "Resilience for Kids & Teens," a school-based campaign that focuses on teaching the skills of resilience for problems ranging from adapting to a new classroom to bullying by classmates or even abuse at home. The campaign included the distribution of a special issue of *Time for Kids* magazine to more than two million fourth- through sixth-graders and their teachers to help children learn the skills of resilience, using "kid-friendly" language." The APA has also partnered with the Discovery Health Channel for a national multimedia campaign designed to help Americans work through personal tragedies by learning strategies for resilience.

Seeking Advice

Many people feel that they must shoulder a difficult situation themselves; it's somehow dishonorable to lean on others. But in fact, seeking advice is a very useful coping strategy. Sometimes, just talking with someone close can help you think through your situation; at other times, expert advice may be needed.

Renee, a factory worker, received a note from her husband saying that he had packed up and left. She couldn't believe that she had been abandoned; she had little money and three children to support. She felt utterly empty, "as if someone had taken my insides and torn them out of me." As she sat in front of me with tears in her eyes, recalling that moment, I asked, "How did you survive?" "My situation was unbelievable," she answered. "It was out of my control, stressful, horrible. But I had two things going for me. First, I had the support of three kids who comforted me at the beginning and pushed me to take a secretarial course so I could get a better job. Second, I became good at finding resources, like the lawyer who helped me for no money. My ability to seek advice helped me find the counselor who told me to join a support group and to keep a diary of everything that was said." Knowing how to seek advice and uncover resources is critical for coping with a situation that needs changing.

Asserting Yourself

The skill of asserting yourself effectively can help you through daily hassles as well as major transitions. For example, Joan, a shy young woman, felt "put upon" because Amy, her roommate, expected Joan to type her papers. Grateful for Amy's friendship and afraid of losing it, Joan did the typing but with great resentment.

After a course on assertiveness training at a local recreation center, Joan learned how to empathize with Amy: "I understand your need to have papers typed." But she also learned how to say no: "However, typing your papers makes me feel resentful, something I don't think is good for our relationship. Why don't you hire a typist?"

This strategy is so much better than screaming, "You always impose on me and I'm sick of it!" Learning to say no without feeling guilty can add an important skill to your coping repertoire and your mental health.

Brainstorming a New Plan

When faced with a challenging situation, many people feel trapped and stymied because they lack new ways of problem solving. Sometimes it helps to brainstorm, alone or with someone else. You simply let your ideas flow, generating all the suggestions or solutions you can think of, without censoring them or judging whether they make sense or could really work. After you note as many suggestions as you can generate, then you sit down and think carefully through the pros and cons of each one. The important thing is to turn off your critical judgment at first, so your ideas can develop.

I was very surprised a few years ago when James and Deb, casual friends of my husband, invited us to brunch. I was even more surprised when the purpose became clear. Before we ate, they showed us their apartment, tastefully decorated. At brunch James announced that he had been very depressed about his dead-end job; in fact, he felt on the verge of suicide.

We both listened sympathetically as he and his wife described their desperation, the continual appointments with new psychiatrists, and the medications that never seemed to help. Finally, they explained, they had decided to invite people over to explore new directions he might take in his career.

We suggested a number of options, including volunteer work. Every one met with responses like "That's a good idea, but it's not practical" or "That really doesn't interest me." We were stymied; they had asked for our help and our empathic listening, yet they had not really wanted either.

Finally I commented on how frustrating our inability to help must feel to them. Then I pointed out how creative they had been in decorating their bedroom. The bed, for example, had been placed in the center of the room, not against the wall. They agreed that it was an offbeat arrangement and said that they had tried many others before hitting on this.

Something clicked in my head. I suggested that since they had solved a decorating problem by being willing to explore many options, the same approach might work in thinking about James's career. Somehow this hit home. They acknowledged their resistance, and we began to brainstorm together in earnest, developing a long list of career options for James to consider—some wild and improbable, some very conventional. I recently learned that he is in a completely new line of work and loves it.

I am not suggesting that there are always unlimited opportunities to be or do anything you choose. Remember when women couldn't be astronauts; when blacks couldn't be college presidents, except at black institutions; when homosexuals couldn't hold high government positions; and when people over sixty-five couldn't hold jobs in most organizations? Although at times certain options really are closed, there are usually many ways to manage and create opportunities if we just let ourselves imagine them.

Brian's story puts it all in perspective. In one disastrous moment, a car accident transformed Brian, an athletic young man, into a paraplegic. At first he wanted to give up and die. "What's the use of living?" he asked himself. Then he became angry, at himself for falling asleep at the wheel, and at "God" for letting this happen to him. Eventually, he began to fight to stay alive and to find meaning in his life. But it didn't happen overnight.

It took a year of hard work before Brian was able to leave the hospital and move home. It took another year to become accustomed to a whole new routine—doing hours of physical exercise each day, learning how to manipulate a wheelchair and how to drive a car. During that year he broke up with his lover and moved out on his own.

In addition to concentrating on managing his body and his day-to-day living, Brian needed to figure out what to do with his life. He had been a carpenter working for a building contractor; clearly he could no longer do that. What other options did he have? At first he felt he had none—that his life was over. He realized that he could live his life as a loser and a victim or he could, as he wrote his mother, "face my future with hope, courage, and curiosity." What changes could he initiate that would make his life meaningful?

The answer came on a ten-hour plane trip to the National Conference for the Disabled, when Brian discovered that planes have no space for wheelchairs to fit into toilets. As a result, he had a very humiliating experience on that flight. But that experience convinced him that architects must understand the problems of the disabled. He decided then to explore becoming an architect, interior designer, or draftsman so he could help others like himself. He used brainstorming with friends and his family about how to make this happen. Eventually, he enrolled in a doctoral counseling program, deciding he would rather help people directly, but his activism helped promote legislation that we now have—making all public places accessible for everyone.

Brian had survived a horrible accident; he had broken up a long-standing relationship; and he developed a plan for a new, useful career. Although his body is not whole, he is a whole person. He created, uncovered, and discovered sides to himself that he never knew he had and options that he had never imagined. This is not meant to romanticize tragedy but merely to point out the endlessly possible ways to live a life.

STRATEGIES TO CHANGE THE MEANING OF THE TRANSITION

There are times when you simply can't change a situation: you didn't receive tenure, your plant closed, your best friend moved away, you have suffered a debilitating accident. As one woman wrote:

"We recently retired. I wanted part-time work but nobody was knocking on my door. My husband was depressed about money. He wanted to sell our large house and move to a less expensive community. One day my daughter said she understood my being upset because of what it represented. Our move was triggered by negatives—with decreased incomes we could no longer afford our house, we did not need so much space, we were questioning what we would do in retirement. We were in a period of feeling loss and less, not more and hope.

"When my daughter responded that 'it was because of what it represented' I began crying. She held me, said nothing. I felt better. Someone knew, someone heard. I was then able to reframe—I still had a living husband I loved, friends, and some possibilities. By reframing—changing the meaning of the transition—I could see the challenges and possibilities."

There are many *Strategies* to consider using when you seem to be up against a brick wall.

Applying Knowledge of the Transition Process

One of the basic tenets of this book is that transitions alter your life and require a period of adjustment—often several years. Remember the story about Melissa and Frank's move into a condominium? They sold the family home and moved into a condo before their son had left home and before they had originally expected to do it.

Some of the difficulty arose because the timing was bad for their son. But even with better planning and timing, the move would have been disruptive because the beginning of any transition is quite stressful. They needed to understand that their reactions were quite normal, that we *all* feel confused any time our *routines* and *assumptions* are changed.

Remember Lisa, who moved to take a great new job and join her lover? A year after the move she was depressed and still couldn't get her feelings together, despite all the pluses. Lisa's case raises a critical point. When a major disruption occurs, the transition process requires a great deal of adaptation, even when the benefits far outweigh the deficits. In other words, even though the move was positive, Lisa had still changed her daily and monthly *routines*, her worker *role*, and some of her *assumptions* about herself. Transitions are usually much easier for people who have ample coping resources than they are for people with very limited resources. But people in both situations can be helped by knowing about the transition process. Of course, the process and its pain are still there, but understanding can cut down on some of the upset.

I am reminded of a widow who had abruptly moved to an area where she knew no one and where driving was a necessity, although she had no license. She later said she wished someone had told her that there would be an end to the agony of bereavement. It wouldn't have eased the pain or the mourning over her husband's death, but it would have been comforting to know that someday she would move past the despair she felt. She realized too late that her hasty decision to move was not helpful.

In other words, knowledge of the transition process can ease one's pain and provide a perspective that today is not forever. It helps to incorporate the information from chapters 1 and 2 about transitions and the transition process.

Rehearsing the Transition

The late sociologist Bernice Neugarten described the importance of rehearsing for transitions—trying to visualize exactly how you would behave if an expected transition occurred. For example, men often rehearse for retirement and women for widowhood.[7]

Rehearsing includes thinking about, even discussing, one's projected transition. It involves questions such as, for example, where will you live when you retire? What will you wear when you get up in the morning? How will you structure your day? Such rehearsals help people cope with the events when they really happen. It is harder to deal with transitions when they are "off-time"—for example, when retirement comes early because of an unexpected plant closing, or when a young spouse is accidentally killed—partly because people don't rehearse for such situations. An increasing number of people who retire to the Sun Belt rehearse the move by living in their new locale for a winter before relocating there permanently.

Developing Rituals

Transitions are sometimes easier to accept when they are accompanied by rituals. Weddings, christenings, and farewell parties are all rituals that ease our transitions. But many important transitions do not have established rituals, and people may have to create their own. The importance of rituals can be seen in the story of Janet, who at age eighteen announced to her parents that instead of staying at home and attending the local junior college, she had decided to go to work and move into her own apartment.

Her shocked parents felt rejected. They had given her a good home. Why was she leaving it? And how would they cope with this unexpected transition? There was no accepted ritual to help them deal with having an eighteen-year-old move out of the house.

Coincidentally, Janet's parents heard the late anthropologist Barbara Myerhoff discuss the importance of ritual in helping people deal with "marginal periods"—when they are shifting from one phase of life to another. She described the many significant events and nonevents that we fail to ritualize. She even used the case of eighteen-year-olds moving out.

Janet's parents took Myerhoff's presentation seriously and decided to ritualize Janet's departure by giving a celebration dinner and inviting their closest family friends. They chose gifts and wrote poems to commemorate her past and celebrate her future. They even promised to pay for phone installation in Janet's apartment, which would connect Janet to her past—but they expected her to pay the monthly phone charges. This helped them all handle the transition.

Myerhoff taught people how to develop rituals that "punctuate and clarify" critical times in their lives. The divorce ritual in the film *Rites of Renewal* does just that.[8] The minister called together the divorcing couple, asking them to pledge their care, concern, and love for their children even though their love for each other had vanished. He also included the couple's parents and friends in the ceremony. Many cry while watching this film. It probably reminds us of times when we have experienced such wrenching splits.

Making Positive Comparisons ("Count Your Blessings")

People tend to judge the severity of their situations by comparing them with the situations of others. Blanche, a woman in a nursing home who had Lou Gehrig's disease (an illness that eventually obliterates all muscle function), could barely talk or swallow. She had lost all movement of her arms and legs. But one day she said to me, "Bad as this is, at least I don't have to be tube fed."

Psychologist Shelley Taylor studied the reactions women had to their breast cancer. Most of the women "chose to compare themselves to other patients who were . . . more seriously ill. When patients did not know an actual person who was worse off, they invented an imaginary one. For example, patients who had one lump removed pitied women who had undergone full mastectomies. . . . Even women who were very seriously ill found relief in the knowledge that they were not dying or were not in pain." The point "is that they make . . . comparisons."[9]

Rearranging Priorities

One way to change the meaning of a difficult transition is to define the aspect of your life in which you are stressed as less important to you than other aspects of your life. A person frustrated in a job area may decide that love, family, and community service are what really matter and that work is just a way to earn a living. If the stress is in the family area, then work may become a top priority.

Some of the men my colleagues and I interviewed whose jobs had been eliminated were devastated because their work was critical to their sense of selfhood. They were unable to devalue the job and play up some other aspects of their lives. But one of the men, a grass cutter, said that his job was not that important to him. In fact, he said, if he didn't work, his wife would go back to being a cook and he would care for the children—an activity he had always enjoyed.

Redefining priorities often happens spontaneously as a way of coping. It's harder to do it deliberately, but it can be done if you step back mentally from the stressful situation and try to see which other areas of your life also matter a lot to you. One way to size up their importance is to ask yourself how you'd feel if they, too, were severely disrupted.

Relabeling: The Process of Redefining the Transition

Richard Lazarus and Susan Folkman found that as individuals size up and label their current situation as irrelevant, positive, or stressful, they also assess their ability and resources to cope with the situation. But these labels can be changed. Relabeling occurs when you redefine either the situation or your ability to cope with it.

Earlier, I described the celebration ritual for Janet, the young woman who moved into her own apartment—a transition her parents had initially viewed as very stressful. After listening to an anthropologist's speech, Janet's parents relabeled the transition as positive;

instead of regarding Janet's departure as a rejection, they started to see it as part of growing up.

Forgiving

I interviewed Daniel, the CEO of a large company. He spoke with real authority. I remember thinking in a stereotypical way, "He's a real man." After a short time he shifted the conversation to his parents, to how they shortchanged him, how they verbally abused him, and how they forced him to follow a business rather than an artistic path. It was sad to hear this fifty-year-old man still so upset by his parents that he could not forgive them. The title of chapter 1 in psychologist Robert Enright's book *Forgiveness Is a Choice* says it all: "Forgiveness: A Path to Freedom." Daniel was consumed with his parents; he was not free. To forgive, according to Enright, is not to forget. It is to acknowledge that we are angry, maybe resentful, for the hurt we feel resulting from another person's actions toward us. Acknowledging to ourselves our right to be angry frees us to forgive but not necessarily forget.

By not forgiving his parents, Daniel was stuck in a childlike reaction. His inner life and outer appearance were out of sync. To become fully mature, Daniel needed to go through a process of forgiveness. According to Enright, you first need to acknowledge your anger and commit to forgive as a way to "release [yourself] from emotional prison."[10]

Selective Ignoring

Some people use "selective ignoring" to help them cope. When faced with a troublesome situation, they may play down the bad parts and play up the good. Many partnerships flounder because one partner notices every bad habit of the other. After two divorces, one man reported that counseling had helped him realize that he had focused on all the negative habits of his former wives. He began to see that focusing on the positives and not looking for perfection makes for a much better relationship. This strategy, however, is easier said than done. It can be learned and added to your repertoire—as the story of Beth, the single mother of two teenagers, illustrates.

Beth knows she is a "direct-action" person. If something goes wrong, she negotiates and asserts herself. If she needs help, she'll call everyone she knows to find the appropriate resource. Her coping style has helped her through many difficult times, but it has sometimes backfired.

When Sherry, her sixteen-year-old daughter, started driving, Beth was always on her case. If Sherry came home one minute late, Beth would be at the door, almost pouncing on her. This inevitably provoked a fight and failed to encourage Sherry's promptness. Then Beth learned about "selective ignoring." She decided to try it out.

Clearly, Beth cannot and should not ignore a lateness of two hours. But ten minutes is another story. By deliberately not "noticing" everything, Beth is giving a message of confidence to Sherry. But more important, Beth has added another *Strategy* to her coping repertoire.

Beth reported that all was going well until Rick, her fourteen-year-old son, perceived that his mother was being more lenient with Sherry. Then Rick started nagging Beth, accusing her of being too easy on his sister. Beth concluded her story with a laugh, saying, "You never can win!"

Denial

We have grown up thinking that good mental health and facing reality go hand in hand. Lately, though, a surge of research has been pointing out that some types of denial can be beneficial.

Psychiatrist George Vaillant distinguishes between *immature* and *mature* denial. In immature denial, for instance, people redefine external reality in a false way by saying, when someone needs an operation, that surgery has no risks. In mature denial, people make a "conscious or semi-conscious decision to postpone paying attention" to a problem or reality. They are "postponing but not avoiding forever" dealing head-on with the problem.[11]

For some people, going into surgery armed with all the facts can lead to unnecessary anxiety. They might be more comfortable finding out what they need to know about the surgeon's competence but not every detail—every risk and consequence—before the operation. Later, they will be in a better position to handle the information.

Humor

When my colleagues and I interviewed people about how they cope, most of them did not spontaneously mention using humor as a strategy. But when we specifically asked about their use of humor, many could remember a time when it had worked. I asked members of a group, "Have you ever used humor as a way to cope?" One person said, "Always! It helps to be able to see the silly, negative, stupid things I have done to contribute to a bad situation." Or to verbalize extremes. These extremes often lurk in your mind as fears, and turning them into humor depowers them. Humor helps you interpret a situation in a new way and treat embarrassing or dangerous emotions in a less emotionally charged way. A number of strategies can be used to "improve your laugh life." You can think of situations, books, and movies that make you laugh out loud. You can look at the humor in what you are doing—try to laugh at yourself.

Having Faith

Many of us find it important to reflect about ourselves, our world, and our place in it. We meditate, pray, read, and visit churches, temples, mosques—even psychics. Several recent articles have reported on stockbrokers, government officials, and others who visit psychics for a reading on a regular basis. One woman wrote, "I think for many people God and their faith is an important part of their lives and can influence how they behave and perceive things. From my perspective, life doesn't end at death but goes on forever."

On a recent cross-country plane trip I was sitting beside a woman who was reading her Bible. She told me her story. Her husband was in the Navy; she has moved at least fifteen times since they married. I asked how she felt about moving, and she said she loves it. "It's really a challenge—it keeps me stretched." "How do you deal with all the changes?" I asked. She explained that until about six years ago she had lived her married life always trying to please everyone. If her husband yelled at her—and he often did—she wouldn't yell back. Even in the grocery line, she would try to please the cashier. She hated being so insecure.

Then she had "a conversation with Jesus" that changed her life. She began to worry less about her own insecurity and began to approach people differently. Christ told her that her marriage was stagnant and that much of the problem was her own inability to be herself and be direct. She participated more in church and began to speak up more at home.

Finally she told her husband that while she did not expect him to change, she did expect him to accept her change. Since he did not seem able to do that, she decided to leave him. He was so astounded by this that he, too, joined the church, and their marriage was renewed. He no longer loses his temper, she said; he is now a better administrator in the Navy and a much better husband and father. She feels that she can handle anything now because of her relationship with God and Jesus Christ. That feeling gave her the strength to make a radical change in her view of herself and in her subsequent behavior.

Another woman, whose faith helped her cope, explained her situation this way: "I was dealing with parents, in-laws, two adult children, a demanding husband, and my own desire to work. The pressures became great when my mother became critically ill and I had to travel frequently across the country, sometimes staying with her for weeks at a time. I managed by remembering how I had coped when my father-in-law was ill. I remembered that the way I did it was to take each day at a time, relying on faith. My religious beliefs are strong and very important to me. I realized that the life course is one in which there is an expectation of death, that I, too, will die. I just kept thinking how fulfilled my mother's life had been, how happy I was that I was well and could help her."

TAKING STRESS IN YOUR STRIDE: MANAGING REACTIONS TO STRESS

We have looked at strategies that help you change your situation or change its meaning. But how do you deal with stress when it seems impossible to change or redefine the situation that is the source of your stress? As you become more conscious of the effects of stress, you will learn to use strategies that help you relax so you can take the stress in stride. I will describe a number of strategies that people use, but you may have to experiment to find the ones that work best for you. Reading, for example, can be relaxing for one person but agitating for another. And to further complicate things, what relaxes you at one time in your life or during one transition can stress you at another time.

In response to a questionnaire asking people how they cope with stressful situations, one respondent said, "I went into therapy, made new friends, attended a health spa for aerobics and massages, took a program in progressive relaxation and self-hypnosis, joined a singles group for support, and started doing fun things like dancing." The list of possible strategies is extremely varied: playing; reading; using relaxation skills; meditating; imaging; using biofeedback; expressing emotions (through praying, crying, laughing, singing, chanting); relaxing through massage and visiting spas; and engaging in physical exercise such as jogging, swimming, aerobics, and dancing.

Playing

We normally think of playing as the province of children and gods and forget how crucial it is for adults. Dan Leviton, a former professor at the University of Maryland and director of the Adult Health and Development Activity program for older adults, reported that fun and play are among the best buffers to stress. He had designed a simple but effective program to teach people how to play.

Each older person in the program is teamed with an undergraduate. Together they participate in enjoyable activities such as singing, dancing, and listening to lectures. My colleagues and I interviewed some of the older adults in his program. One man reported that he had been at the end of his rope. First his wife had died, then his only son. Somehow he had heard of the program, dragged himself over to the university, and to his amazement started having fun and feeling again that he could find enjoyment and pleasure in his life. As he said, "The program literally saved my life."

People sometimes get so caught up in the strain of a transition that they forget to build fun and pleasure into their lives, or they feel they don't have time for fun. It may be impossible to go on your dream vacation, but there are many simpler, more accessible pleasures that are fun and that can help you to relax. One woman goes hat shopping when she needs a fun break. Another takes luxurious bubble baths. A neighbor gets some friends together for a round of poker. A cousin hits the road to explore the local antique shops. If you think about it, you can come up with your own roster of small pleasures that are fun to do and that can fit into your most stressful period.

Emotional Release

Transitions often generate powerful emotional reactions: anxiety, joy, anger, frustration, sadness, and more. Yet, there's a strong streak of "stiff-upper-lip" philosophy in our culture that makes it hard for some people to deal with such feelings. They try to stifle them but often find later that they surface in surprisingly inappropriate ways. The problem is particularly severe for some men, who—despite an onslaught of articles telling them it's okay to experience emotions and even to cry—still feel it's unmanly to reveal that they're upset.

It is useful to label our emotional reactions that accompany our transitions. Clearly, we use a range of emotions as we face the ups and downs of life. We often have multiple reactions, but labeling them can help diffuse them. Psychologist Richard Lazarus categorizes emotions as:

- Those that result from a goal being blocked—or the "Nasty Emotions"—such as anger or hostility;
- Those that result from a goal being attained such as happiness, joy, pride, love;
- "Existential Emotions" that reflect ambiguity such as anxiety, fright, guilt, shame, sadness, depression; or
- "Empathetic Emotions" such as gratitude and compassion.[12]

Whatever the emotion you are experiencing, it can be helpful to talk to a spouse, close friend, or therapist as a way to let off some emotional "steam" constructively.

Counseling, Therapy, and Support

Counseling, therapy, and the support of people close to you can help you manage stress, change the meaning of the situation, or change the situation. A few examples show how counseling and support help people manage a stressful period.

It was wonderful to see my college roommate, Joan, after thirty-five years. We started talking and joking as if we had never been apart. She quickly caught me up on the good things in her life. She was still married to Bill, whom she had met in college, and they had three fine children. He had done well as an accountant, and she was working as a social worker.

Then she talked at length about the unexpected depression she had just conquered. It had started after a very stressful year, when her mother died, her best friend moved to California, and she stuck by two good friends as they succumbed slowly to cancer. Then her eldest daughter had had a big wedding, which Joan orchestrated.

Joan began to feel depressed after the wedding, and soon depression seemed to consume her. Instead of focusing on all her separations and losses, Joan became obsessed with her husband's close friendship with Sylvia, a friend of hers. She began feeling that her husband paid more attention to Sylvia, even to their dog, than to her. All in all, it was a horrible period; she feared she was going crazy.

I asked Joan what helped her cope. Her immediate answer was, "Friends and a therapist." Her friends assured her that Bill would never stray and that Sylvia flirted with all their husbands. She loved hearing Bill defended and Sylvia criticized.

Her therapist helped her realize that she needed more time to mourn the many changes in her life. She appreciated the therapist's giving her "permission" to be depressed. Together, the comments of friends and her therapist reassured her that she might be overreacting, but she wasn't crazy.

We can see how interrelated counseling and support are. In fact, counseling is sometimes a temporary support for people in transition.

Other Strategies

Many techniques such as biofeedback, imaging, and relaxation tapes are designed to help people control their physical reactions to stressful situations. For example, migraine headaches can sometimes be eased through biofeedback. Some claim that imaging—a technique for visualizing clearly in your mind a desired effect—can assist in fighting cancer, and others claim it can produce weight loss.

Relaxation tapes are often used before surgery. One man who had been afraid to admit his fear of surgery was grateful when a friend brought him a tape player and some music cassettes. The friend also slipped in a relaxation tape, which he found very soothing.

Reading can both distract and instruct. Self-help books, novels, plays, and advice columns can all help at different times. When asked to describe a positive transition in his life, one man answered, "I realized I was gay." In describing how he coped with this transition, he explained, "I pretty much handled it by myself. I couldn't turn to my family or friends because I thought they would reject me. I read a lot of material in libraries and in bookstores about homosexuality. I realized through reading that I was like a lot of other people and not simply alone."

Jogging, swimming, aerobics, walking, tennis, dancing, and other forms of physical activity have many purposes. They are fun; they drain off excess energy; and they redirect one's concentration away from whatever is worrisome.

The manager of a condominium who was caught in a cross fire of complaints from residents and management reported, "I was going out of my mind." Then she started jogging. Both her figure and her mental health improved. She now jogs regularly and feels "100 percent better."

USING MANY COPING *STRATEGIES*

There is no one magic way to cope, but there are many possible *Strategies* to consider and try. In addition to using *Strategies* that change your situation or your way of looking at it, you might try to relax and take your stress in stride. Table 5.1 will enable you to TAKE STOCK of which ones you now use.

In the next chapter, as you TAKE CHARGE, you will identify which new ones you might like to try. Remember, it's not the com-

TABLE 5.1.   YOUR COPING STRATEGIES WORKSHEET

Possible Coping Strategies	Now Using
• Taking action to change or modify the transition	
Negotiating	❑
Taking optimistic action	❑
Seeking advice	❑
Asserting yourself	❑
Brainstorming a new plan	❑
Taking legal action (if needed)	❑
• Changing the meaning of the transition	
Applying knowledge of the transition process	❑
Rehearsing	❑
Developing rituals	❑
Making positive comparisons	❑
Rearranging priorities	❑
Relabeling or reframing	❑
Selectively ignoring	❑
Using denial	❑
Using humor	❑
Having faith	❑
• Managing Reactions to Stress	
Playing	❑
Using relaxation skills	❑
Expressing emotions	❑
Doing physical activity	❑
Participating in counseling, therapy, or support groups	❑
Reading	❑
• Doing nothing	
• Other Strategies	

Source: Based on work from L. I. Pearlin and C. Schooler, "The Structure of Coping," *Journal of Health and Social Behavior* 19 (1978): 2–21. Reprinted with permission.

mitment to a particular strategy that makes the difference; it's the commitment to mobilizing your resources, to trying new things, and "hanging in there, baby!" In the next chapter, we'll look more specifically at how to choose the strategies that are best suited to your particular situation.

As one woman who was widowed wrote: "I discovered that I used many coping strategies. Giving in to my sad feelings helped me get through them. I jogged every day, which helped me reduce the stress. I talked to myself, reassuring myself that things would get better and that I could handle the situation. I also talked to trusted others and learned it was more helpful to be listened to than rescued. The emotional pain made the world look gray and bleak, but I felt that the pain lifted, and with it, my spirit, when I was able to have a sense of humor. Although not changing anything, it did provide temporary relief. The process took time; there were many setbacks. I discovered that there is no 'best' coping strategy that works in all situations, but no matter how difficult the situation, I will eventually find a way to cope with it."

YOUR COPING *STRATEGIES* REVIEW

- Do you use a range of strategies?   Yes   No
- Do you sometimes take action to change the transitions?   Yes   No
- Do you sometimes try to change the meaning of the transitions?   Yes   No
- Do you try to take stress in stride?   Yes   No
- Do you know when to do nothing?   Yes   No
- Do you feel that you can flexibly choose different strategies depending on the challenge at hand?   Yes   No

- Taking all of the above into account, do you
  rate your *Strategies* as:

A high resource?	Yes	No
A low resource?	Yes	No
A mixed bag?	Yes	No
Okay?	Yes	No

TAKING CHARGE

Now for the BIG question: What can you do about your own particular situation?

The third and last section of this book shifts the focus to your own plan, showing how to turn your vulnerabilities into strengths, enabling you to cope with transitions more effectively. Every transition cannot be turned into an inspirational success, but every person can be helped to master change, whether you are like Jamil (who moved to a new city for the "perfect" job and after a year is still depressed), Mary (who is caught between an aging mother and two adult "children"), or the mother of two teenage children on drugs, who totally lost confidence in herself as a parent. You can learn how to handle your reactions. In other words, surviving a transition doesn't guarantee that one will also profit from it. By talking with those who have negotiated their transitions successfully and profited from change, I discovered some survival tips. One man reported having great feelings of hopelessness throughout two years in a job search. After that period, he concluded, "If I can weather that, I can weather anything. I will never be that upset again. In addition, I have more understanding of what one goes through after one loses a job and before one gets another one. Patience is key!"

The tips given all through the book do not guarantee a fairy-tale ending to a transition. As I pointed out when describing the transition process, reactions to transitions change over time. At one point, a transition might seem "for worse" and at another point "for better." Life for most people really is a series of ups and downs. We know that one can be as overwhelmed with a sought-after life change as with a dreaded one. It is not the event or non-event that makes the difference—it is what we do with it that counts. I believe that we have profited from change when we feel we have more options than we did before, when we have increased our understanding of the underlying and recurring issues that accompany any transition, when we have increased our feeling that we can control and take charge of our lives and that we are open to learn from others.

We can learn from others in the following chapters. Chapter 6 presents a general framework for taking action, no matter what the transition; chapter 7, a new chapter, deals with taking charge of your non-event transitions; chapter 8, an expanded chapter, describes how work and family transitions are linked; and chapter 9 provides an opportunity for you to apply all you have learned to your own transitions.

6

YOUR ACTION PLAN FOR MASTERING CHANGE

Some time ago I delivered a speech on coping to middle managers of a major corporation. After describing the 4 S's—*Situation*, *Self*, *Supports*, and *Strategies*—and the four major categories of coping strategies—taking action to change the transition, changing the meaning of the transition, managing reactions to stress, and choosing to do nothing—I felt I had covered everything the attendees needed to know about change. However, the first question proved me wrong. "How do I know when to use a particular strategy?" asked someone from the audience. This challenge resulted in the following Action Plan for Mastering Change.

The Action Plan combines the coping strategies with the 4 S's to help ease the agonies of change, to neutralize and solve problems, and to turn liabilities into resources. By implementing the steps in sequence, you will see how modifying one or more of the 4 S's can help you traverse a transition with more creativity and control than otherwise may have seemed possible.

At a recent workshop, one man expressed concern about people who do not think in such systematic ways and who rely more on intuition than on a step-by-step plan. His concern is legitimate. I too have often thought that step-by-step plans take the romance and surprise out of living. However, I can think of nothing more romantic than dancing. Yet, to dance well and with freedom, one needs to know the steps. Eventually, a good dancer improvises. Similarly, this system of TAKING STOCK and TAKING CHARGE of change is not meant to hem you in. On the contrary, once you know some basic steps and techniques, you'll be in a position to improvise your own plan. This chapter provides a framework for empowering you to help yourself. In other words, when you have a knowledge and skill base, you are freed to innovate, experiment, and improvise.

WEATHERING CHANGE

We are often weathering change, some of which is out of our control. We will revisit Carolyn, George, and Esther to learn from them—to see how they weathered change and what tips they can offer us.

Carolyn's Four S's: TAKING STOCK

When we met Carolyn in chapter 1, she was trying to cope with multiple transitions—a new marriage, a move away from family and church, and a tubal pregnancy. She was APPROACHING a transition that had changed most aspects of her life. Carolyn's challenge was to figure out what to do about a seemingly endless, miserable forever.

In assessing her *Situation*, we are reminded that it's important to consider the type of transition, whether or not it is having a major impact on the person's life, and the degree to which the person experiencing it feels in control.

Carolyn was facing multiple transitions. Any one of them would have been enough to throw many people for a loop. Cut off from her friends, her relatives, and her church at a time of multiple transitions, she could see immediately that her *Situation* offered little more than "low" ratings. Her combination of transitions clearly added up to a "biggie": her new relationship with her husband and the loss of her old stable relationships in her hometown; the change imposed on her routine by geographical isolation; the occurrence of the problem pregnancy at a time when she was already under pressure; and her newness both to marriage and to the area where she was living. This resulted in low marks on all her coping resources. As she said, "If you had a ten-point scale and ten was miserable, I'd be off the scale."

Carolyn's own words show how she felt about her *Self.* She lacked a sense of well-being and self-knowledge and was generally pessimistic. When we first saw Carolyn, she was sitting at home and crying. She felt bereft of support. Her husband felt that she was withdrawing from him, and he was confused; she was unable to relate to him as an adult. She had never been separated from her family before and blamed her husband for her feelings of isolation. Carolyn was simultaneously facing the issues of how to create intimacy with a new husband and how to cope with separation from her family. At the time we first interviewed her, she would have rated her *Supports* as low.

Reviewing Carolyn's coping *Strategies,* it became evident that she was using few if any of them. She was "doing nothing"—but not out of choice. She didn't know what to do. She just stayed home feeling overwhelmed.

Carolyn's 4 S Worksheet (see table 6.1) helps us visualize her coping resources.

Carolyn's Action Plan

Carolyn's multiple transitions added up to the serious challenge of low ratings in all four areas. Not only was she facing a very trying series of changes, but she was obviously not well equipped to deal with them.

TABLE 6.1. CAROLYN TAKES STOCK—HER 4 S WORKSHEET

APPROACHING CHANGE

- *Type:* <u>Multiple</u>
- *Impact on roles, relationships, routines, assumptions:* <u>Major</u>

TAKING STOCK OF YOUR COPING RESOURCES

Ratings	*High*	*Okay*	*Low*
• *Your Situation*: overall			X
Your evaluation			X
Timing			X
Control			X
Previous experience			X
Other stress			X
• *Your Self:* overall			X
Response to transition (optimist, pessimist)			X
Sense of well-being (mastery and pleasure)			X
Self-knowledge			X
• *Your Supports:* overall			X
Getting affection, affirmation, aid			X
Evaluation—getting enough and the right mixture			X
Interrupted by transition			X
• *Your Coping Strategies:* overall			X
Taking action to change or modify your Situation, Supports, Self, Strategies			X
Changing the way you see the transition			X
Managing your reactions to transition			X
Doing nothing			
Other			

Yet, after a year she felt that she had come through the worst, was no longer a complete outsider, and could start to build a satisfying new life. How did this happen?

Although Carolyn could not see how to change her *Situation*, she knew that she needed help. One day while she was in the doctor's office the physician's assistant, Molly, noticed how depressed she seemed to be and began to draw her out. When Molly showed empathy with Carolyn's distress about having a pregnancy far away from home, Carolyn began to cry. Molly, trained as a physician's assistant, was taking a graduate degree in social work. She immediately realized how vulnerable Carolyn was and also guessed rightly that Carolyn would not seek help from a professional. Molly suggested that Carolyn come in to talk with her for half an hour before her regular appointments with the doctor. Carolyn did so, and during these sessions she was able to seek Molly's advice about what to do, how to meet people, and how to break out of her depression.

As Carolyn confided in and discussed her *Situation* with the caring, competent Molly, she was able to devise several *Strategies* that eventually helped her turn the tide to get her on the road back to health and optimism.

Carolyn's Action Plan (see table 6.2) summarizes the *Strategies* she used to strengthen her resources.

TABLE 6.2.　CAROLYN TAKES CHARGE

Possible Coping Strategies	*Strengthening Your 4 S's*
Taking Action to Change or Modify Your 4 S's	
Negotiating	Negotiating with husband for use of car and regular long-distance calls to family
Taking optimistic action	Joined church group and newcomers club
	(continued)

TABLE 6.2. (CONTINUED)

Possible Coping Strategies	Strengthening Your 4 S's
Seeking advice	Later started outreach program for others
Asserting yourself	Enrolled in assertiveness training
Brainstorming a new plan	
Taking legal action	
Other	

Changing the Way You See Things

Applying knowledge of the transition process	Learned that transitions take time and that she could begin to control the outcomes
Developing rituals	
Making positive comparisons	
Rearranging priorities	
Reappraising, relabeling, refraining	From assertiveness training, she learned to feel "entitled" to support, car, etc.
Ignoring selectively	
Denying	
Having faith	
Other	

Managing Your Reactions to the Transition

Playing	Began to socialize with other couples
Using relaxation skills	
Expressing emotions	
Engaging in physical activity	Joined exercise class
Participating in counseling, therapy, or support groups	Became involved in church group, helped work with others who had similar problems of shyness, isolation
Reading	
Other	

Doing Nothing

Using Other Strategies

Carolyn changed her *Situation* by a combination of seeking advice, negotiating, taking optimistic action, and asserting herself. Before she could relate to new friends and begin to make her marriage work, Carolyn needed to change both her *Self* and her coping *Strategies*. With Molly's encouragement, she enrolled in an assertiveness-training group at a nearby church. This helped her learn ways to ask for what she needed without feeling ashamed. Mostly she changed from feeling "not entitled" to feeling "entitled" to support and attention.

Molly encouraged Carolyn to start developing new *Supports* while retaining her connections to her past, so Carolyn negotiated the use of their limited resources with her husband. She suggested to him—and he agreed—that she could use the car twice a week to attend church and that she could spend some of their limited money for long-distance phone calls to her mother three times a week.

When Carolyn first began to participate in activities at the neighborhood church, she was very shy. But with the constant encouragement of her mother, she "hung in there." She discovered and joined a newcomers club that really served as a support group. Eventually she and another woman started an outreach program for people too shy to attend the church.

Carolyn then began to change the way she interpreted her world. She was helped to understand both her *Situation* and her *Self* differently by reframing. She could not undo the move, the marriage, or the pregnancy, but she was helped to change her perspective and understand her distress. Previously very critical of herself for her inability to cope, Carolyn was helped through the new support group and counseling to understand and accept the difficulty of coping with transitions that seem beyond one's control. Clearly she had been involved in the decision to marry, but she had not been in control of the move or the tubal pregnancy.

Molly helped Carolyn realize that she was not a puppet and that she could learn to control her reactions and become more of an optimist. At first, Carolyn did not believe these new words, but as time passed she began to believe that she could, in fact, gain control over her life.

By acquiring knowledge about the transition process, Carolyn was helped to change the way she viewed her *Situation*. She came to understand several major characteristics of transitions and thus enhanced her ability to flow with them.

Many people ask, "How long will it take to resolve my transition?" Unfortunately, no formula can accurately predict the answer to that question. Some authors outline a specific series of stages that everyone experiences as they go through transitions, but I do not believe that life is that clear-cut. My own research shows that the particular phases and their corresponding lengths of time vary greatly depending on how long it takes one to reshape a new and satisfying life: that is, a new set of *roles*, *relationships*, *routines*, and *assumptions*.

At first Carolyn felt confused, as she was between her new and old *roles* and *routines*, and she had no notion that she could become comfortable in her new ones. But she learned that people shifting from one role (such as from single person to married one) pass through three phases: first, identification with the old role; second, leaving the old role but not yet knowing how to behave in the new one; and third, finally, comfort in the new role.

Carolyn also took steps to manage better her reactions to the transition. She joined a support group in the church, continued to see Molly for three months, and joined an exercise class. She began to have a little fun and relaxation. She even met some people and initiated a social event with spouses.

Carolyn's experience demonstrates that using the 4 S system makes it possible to progress from a feeling of helplessness and defeat to feelings of optimism and hope, thereby transforming trauma into a significant, positive change in one's life.

George, the Man Who Was RIFfed

George was working in a large corporation when the word came down that due to financial losses, there would be a RIF (reduction in force) and 5 percent of the staff would lose employment. "I knew my job was not in jeopardy," he told me. "The RIF had been explained, and our department was exempt. So the day my boss told me we had a meeting with his boss, I was excited, certain I was going to get a new challenge. But at that meeting my boss's boss told me that the RIF *would* affect my job: I would have to leave in six weeks!

"I couldn't make myself talk. I couldn't even make my legs move so I could get out the door. I just sat there, stunned. As I look back at that moment, I can now understand why I was so immobilized. Not long before, my wife had left me for another person and my father had moved in with me after he was diagnosed as having terminal cancer. And here they were telling me I'd lose my job! Not only would I be out of work, but I'd be cut off from the company's theatre group—the center of my social and recreational life."

What was it about George's *Situation* that made him so vulnerable? How could George be helped to turn the tide?

George's 4 S's: TAKING STOCK

As George APPROACHED this transition, he saw his *Situation*—the RIF—as out of his control, as very negative and permanent. In addition, he had many other stresses. The recent departure of his wife for another man and his father's coming to live with him had already taken their toll. The prospect of losing his leisure and social life as well as his job was overwhelming. Clearly, George would rate his *Situation* as "low." But despite his multiple losses (wife, colleagues on the job, theatre group), he still had a few close friends. In addition, his father became a *Support* as well as a drain since he was at home, able to encourage him and help him weather the storm. Also,

TABLE 6.3.   GEORGE TAKES STOCK—HIS 4 S WORKSHEET

APPROACHING CHANGE

- *Type:* <u>Surprise</u>
- *Impact on roles, relationships, routines, assumptions:* <u>Major</u>

TAKING STOCK OF YOUR COPING RESOURCES

Ratings	High	Okay	Low
• *Your Situation:* overall			X
Your evaluation			X
Timing			X
Control		X	
Previous experience			X
Other stress			X
• *Your Self:* overall		X	
Response to transition (optimist, pessimist)			X
Sense of well-being (mastery and pleasure)		X	
Self-knowledge	X		
• *Your Supports:* overall			X
Getting affection, affirmation, aid		X	
Evaluation—getting enough and the right mixture		X	
Interrupted by transition			X
• *Your Coping Strategies:* overall		X	
Taking action to change or modify your Situation, Supports, Self, Strategies		X	
Changing the way you see the transition	X		
Managing your reactions to transition			X

George felt he mattered to his father, and that made George feel useful. So his *Supports* were mixed, but mostly low. (See table 6.3.)

He usually saw himself as optimistic, and he used a variety of coping *Strategies*. During our interview (the week of the RIF) George repeatedly contrasted the positive way he had always seen himself— as a coper—with his current evaluation, saying, "I feel like a loser." We rated his *Self* as "okay," though he clearly felt low at the moment.

George kept saying, "I don't know what to do. I don't know how to cope." However, he continually referred to his past, saying, "I always was the one to tell my friends how to cope. Now I'm stuck." The fact that he had coped in the past was a good predictor that his competency would eventually emerge. We therefore marked *Strategies* as "okay." Despite George's crisis of confidence, he rated his *Situation* as low, his *Supports* as low, but his *Self* and *Strategies* as okay.

George's Action Plan

George's Action Plan focused on his *Situation* and *Supports*. His first task was to figure out how to change his *Situation* and his *Supports*, which were both low. "Do I want to take action?" he asked himself. "And if so, what can I do?"

Second, George asked himself whether he wanted to change the way he viewed his *Situation* or his *Supports*, and whether he could benefit from managing his reactions to the transition. Finally, he considered the option of doing nothing or of devising other methods of coping.

Here's what George did. He enrolled in a support program instituted by his employer to assist employees in obtaining new jobs. At the end of a week-long seminar, George had a resumé, a plan for securing a new job, and a "buddy" from the personnel office to help him identify job leads.

George realized that one of his biggest losses was no longer being able to participate in the theatre group at work. After the shock began to wear off and he began to get his bearings, he spoke to the director of the company theatre group, who personally arranged for George to become involved with a community theatre group. They agreed that George would work with the set designers on the next show. Once that was arranged, George felt much better about his entire *Situation*.

Because George was so distressed, he first focused on *Strategies* for managing his reactions, hoping he could feel calmer and more in control. As a result of belonging to a support group he gained an understanding of the psychological aspects of the RIF experience—that leaving a job involves mourning, as when leaving a loved one. George also sought and received personal counseling that helped him manage his stress. He stopped blaming himself for his failed marriage and stopped seeing himself as a victim. At the end of six weeks, George had accepted a new job with a new organization and was making even more money than before.

George felt very defeated after his wife left him. He kept blaming himself and thinking he must be no good. He was not able to let go of those feelings, but after reading self-help books and talking with friends and a counselor, he began to see that it would take time to get over the failed marriage and his feelings of rejection. George realized that with therapy he might be able to sort out what roles he and his wife had played in the breakup of the marriage and what he might be able to do differently in future relationships. He began to see that he could, with work, get there. George began to say that if he could survive the double loss of wife and job, he could handle anything. Quite apart from his work and recreational problems, George faced another problem. He felt imposed upon by his father. But this matter came into perspective after he saw a television show in which a young man places his father in a nursing home and ends up feeling very guilty. That helped George realize that his caring for his father had helped distract him from his own problems and had helped him maintain a good view of himself. (See table 6.4.)

TABLE 6.4. GEORGE TAKES CHARGE

Possible Coping Strategies	*Strengthening Your 4 S's*
Taking Action to Change or Modify Your 4 S's	
Negotiating	
Taking optimistic action	
Seeking advice	Sought advice from theatre director who arranged for him to work in similar group
Asserting yourself	
Brainstorming a new plan	
Taking legal action	
Other	
Changing the Way You See Things	
Applying knowledge of the transition process	
Developing rituals	
Making positive comparisons	
Rearranging priorities	
Reappraising, relabeling, refraining	Realized that miserable as he was about the breakup of his marriage, he had an opportunity to learn about himself so that the same mistakes would not be made again
Ignoring selectively	
Denying	
Having faith	
Other	
Managing Your Reactions to the Transition	
Playing	
Using relaxation skills	
Expressing emotions	
Engaging in physical activity	

(continued)

TABLE 6.4.   (CONTINUED)

Possible Coping Strategies	Strengthening Your 4 S's
Participating in counseling, therapy, or support groups	Participated in outplacement counseling sponsored by employer and after several weeks found another job. Found counselor and began exploring how to cope with transitions, feelings of failure, and the pain of rejection
Reading	
Other	
Doing Nothing	
Using Other Strategies	

INITIATING CHANGE

Carolyn and George are weathering change that they feel was imposed on them. But what about the decisions you make about whether or not to initiate a transition? Esther's breakup and several cases of people considering retirement illustrate the usefulness of the 4 S System when making decisions about your future.

Breaking Up: Esther's Story

"Leaving a marriage or relationship that is bad for you—or, as is more often the case, *not good* for you—is one of the most difficult of all transitions to make. For me, the transition was to stop going with Barry, to end our two-year exclusive relationship, and to stop spending most of my time with him. I wanted to meet someone with whom I could share my life more fully. It took me a long time to carry out my decision, and sometimes I wavered. Although it was a change I wanted, it was scary. I felt the terror most strongly when I awoke in the morning filled with anxiety about the prospect of being out there, of not having a man in my life (especially when my brother had just started a new romance), of being alone, and worse, of being lonely. But if such reasons were to become the glue of my relationship with Barry, I knew it had better be dismantled.

"I was aware that it was five painful days before Valentine's Day. How could I live through Valentine's Day thinking as I was and saying nothing? I decided to analyze my potential transition according to the Four-S System. I first looked at my possible *Situation*. It is terrifying to end a relationship. People will more readily quit their jobs, part with their money, and give up old friends and even their children than end a bad relationship. (How many people live in quiet desperation with the wrong person because they believe there's nobody else out there?) Striking out alone seemed less terrifying when I considered that I had been through breakups before. True, I had not initiated them. But I remember being relieved when they ended and *never* wanting—when an 'ex' had second thoughts and wanted to get together again—to resume.

"Next, I looked at my *Supports* and external resources: I could tick them off. I liked my job. The first half of a new book I had written had been accepted with enthusiasm. I would soon pay off a ten-year debt to my former husband. I had many friends who are stable and supportive and a church that was a joy to attend. They even sell my other three books at the Book Nook each Sunday, where I am asked often to autograph a copy.

"Finally, I knew without enumerating that my inner resources were stronger than they had ever been. After six years of psychotherapy, my habit of negative thinking had been broken, and I no longer felt depressed or unsure of myself. My life was going in the direction I wanted: I had just passed my annual physical, I was working out four to five times a week, and I even had prospects of fitting into a size 10 bathing suit by summer. I had fulfilled the prophecy of a man I met years ago: 'You will really hit your pace when you reach your early forties.'

"Some odd thoughts popped into my mind. I had a new car that wasn't, like the old one, breaking down every month or so. I knew how to fix, or pay someone to fix, most of the things that broke down in my house. I knew where to find college students to do yard work and other jobs.

"As I understand the Four-S System, you count your pluses in four areas: your *Situation, Self, Supports*, and *Strategies*. You also look for weak spots that can be strengthened. The timing was not good. I would be losing not only a lover but a roommate. I could look for a new roommate, but I had no time to look, nor deal with the distractions roommates invariably present. As for sex and male companionship, there would be little time for that while I had a book to finish.

"I had never fully overcome a deep sense of dependency and need to always have a man in my life. I feared that losing the security of this relationship would keep me from concentrating fully on my book. Could I stay home alone nights writing, knowing nobody would be coming over later to spend the night? Should I wait and break off with Barry *after* my book was finished?

"Questions helped me identify my strengths and weaknesses. The question remained not Should I? But Can I? I decided to do it. On a Sunday afternoon before Valentine's Day, I invited Barry over for a cup of tea (my beverage of choice in a crisis) and told him, 'I want always to be friends with you, but I do not want to continue the relationship we have had.'

"I was ending it because I believed I could have an even better life in the future. I was ending it because I would have a chance to cage the dragon of my dependency. I was ending it because I believe you have to say good-bye before you can say hello."

Esther's 4 S's: TAKING STOCK

As Esther thought about her ability to cope, she realized that over the years she had learned when to take action and when to sit tight and do nothing. She carried out a consistent but sensible exercise regime, went to church regularly, and knew what was going on, as she put it, "inside myself."

Esther assessed her *Situation*, her *Self*, her *Supports*, and her *Strategies* and decided to initiate a change in her relationship with Barry. Her *Situation* for leaving was not ideal because of her work deadline, but it was definitely within her control, so we will give it an overall rating of "okay" (see table 6.5). In terms of her *Self*, Esther had entered psychotherapy, was feeling much better about herself as a person, and saw herself in a positive light. She was also aware that she had great dependency needs that influenced her to attach herself and stick to a man. Her overall rating of *Self is* "high." She discussed her many supportive friends and her church, making a "high" for *Supports*. She also felt she was able to utilize many *Strategies*, making that another "high" resource.

To summarize: Esther's resources for coping with change were mostly high. By TAKING STOCK of these, she realized that she was ready for change, that if she was going to make it, this would be the time to do it. However, she also realized two areas of vulnerability: the timing and her possible dependency needs, which surfaced as a need to always have a "man to rely on."

Esther's Action Plan

Even though Esther's resources outweighed her deficits, she realized that the loss she was initiating would be difficult. She therefore decided to prevent any disasters by actively using many *Strategies*. (See table 6.6.)

First, she took optimistic action and decided to make the break with full awareness of her dependency needs. Then she spent a great deal of energy managing her reactions to the transition. Esther selected a strategy uniquely suited to her—writing. She wrote up her own story in terms of the transition model. This process of writing

TABLE 6.5.   ESTHER TAKES STOCK

APPROACHING CHANGE

- *Type:* Elected
- *Impact on roles, relationships, routines, assumptions:* Medium

TAKING STOCK OF YOUR COPING RESOURCES

Ratings	High	Okay	Low
• *Your Situation:* overall		X	
Your evaluation		X	
Timing		X	
Control			X
Previous experience		X	
Other stress		X	
• *Your Self:* overall	X		
Response to transition (optimist, pessimist)	X		
Sense of well-being (mastery and pleasure)	X		
Self-knowledge	X		
• *Your Supports:* overall	X		
Getting affection, affirmation, aid	X		
Evaluation—getting enough and the right mixture		X	
Interrupted by transition		X	
• *Your Coping Strategies:* overall	X		
Taking action to change or modify your Situation, Supports, Self, Strategies			
Changing the way you see the transition			
Managing your reactions to transition			
Doing nothing			
Other			

TABLE 6.6. ESTHER TAKES CHARGE

Possible Coping Strategies	*Strengthening Your 4 S's*
Taking Action to Change or Modify Your 4 S's	
Negotiating	
Taking optimistic action	Decided to make a break with full awareness of her dependency needs
Seeking advice	
Asserting yourself	
Brainstorming a new plan	
Taking legal action	
Other	
Changing the Way You See Things	
Applying knowledge of the transition process	Awareness of ups and downs that are part and parcel of transitions
Developing rituals	
Making positive comparisons	
Rearranging priorities	
Reappraising, relabeling, refraining	
Ignoring selectively	
Denying	
Having faith	
Other	
Managing Your Reactions to the Transition	
Playing	
Using relaxation skills	Read books about breakups and losses
Expressing emotions	
Engaging in physical activity	Joined hiking club/kept up exercise
Participating in counseling, therapy, or support groups	Became very active in church discussion group
Reading	Read books related to loss
Other	
Doing Nothing	
Using Other Strategies	Wrote her own story as a way to think it through

was therapeutic and reinforced her decision to stick with the breakup. She read books about breakups and losses, keeping in mind that there is no way to live a life without facing loss. Esther also made sure she was involved with supportive friends by regularly attending church and participating in the weekly discussion group for singles. Esther also had a fallback plan: if she felt her dependency needs getting out of hand, she would revisit her therapist.

Esther's case illustrates the importance of planning, even when you initiate a change.

Retirement Decisions—Should I, Shouldn't I?

Retirement, a continuation of your career, is a transition similar to high school, college, or graduate school graduation. Some know exactly what they want to do; others are searching for ways to craft a meaningful life. It is important for you to develop a system to determine if this is the right time for you to retire.[1]

Here are some questions you need to address as you figure out if you are ready.

Question 1. Am I ready to retire?

Amy asked, "Should I retire? What will I do if I retire?" Bea said to her husband Steve, "I am afraid for either of us to retire. Our lives are so consumed with our work." And Jeff asked, "How will I know when it is time?"

These are the questions that plague many baby boomers as they approach retirement. They first square off regarding finances. Many meet periodically with their financial advisers and accountants to figure out when they can afford to retire. I remember meeting with our financial adviser, who was much younger than we were. He figured out that we could live on much less money when we stopped working. I explained that we would need more, not less, money and that I did not plan to have spots on my clothes and wear tennis shoes to the theatre. Even if we know where the money will come from to replace our salary (pensions, savings, retirement plans, etc.), we go through a period of fear—can we make it on what we have? Will we outlive our income? We experience what I call "Income Withdrawal Syndrome" when our paychecks stop.

Question 2: Do you have a passion?

Art, a programmer for a university systemwide campus, loved wine and over the years became quite an aficionado. He embraced retirement as a chance to follow his passion. He now teaches classes in wine, conducts wine tastings for an upscale restaurant bar, and is thoroughly enjoying life.

Stan, an investigative reporter for a major newspaper, was a Sunday painter. He opted for early retirement so that he could follow his passion, art. He began painting every day and, after three years, is having his first one-man show. Now he feels comfortable with his new identity as an artist.

Those with a passion are the lucky ones. Even if there is no passion driving our retirement, we can use our retirement to uncover our hidden passion. We can begin looking at regrets, what we wish we had done. If you feel the urge to uncover your passion, then retirement might be a good option. But there are more questions before you make the leap.

Question 3: Do you have the resources to retire?

There is no cookie-cutter answer, as each individual's needs and values are so unique. But the 4 S System can help.

Marilyn, a burned-out university librarian, needs help figuring out if she has her resources in order so that she can opt for early retirement. After consulting with a career counselor, Marilyn realized that she had always wanted to be a marine biologist. She was scared: How would she continue to provide for her children? Would she be able to concentrate? Could she make it? Was she too old to make a fresh start? By assessing her resources, Marilyn can make a judgment about her readiness for retirement.

What is Marilyn's *Situation* at this time in her life? Is this at a time when most of her ducks are in order? In Marilyn's case, her son was graduating from high school and had a full scholarship to a local university. She no longer felt pressure to stay at the university. As her son was gaining independence, so was she.

What did Marilyn bring of her *Self* to this transition? It is important to find if she felt in control as she faced this transition. Marilyn felt a new sense of optimism. Working with the counselor helped her see that she had options. Marilyn was beginning to have hope that her retirement years could be spent pursuing and working in a new career.

What were her *Supports* at this time? Did Marilyn have the emotional and financial support to make this change? She felt that her pension from the university, plus some savings, would take her through her training. She figured that she would be working for another fifteen years, which would give her the financial flexibility she needed. In addition, Marilyn had met with the counselors at the school she planned to attend. There was a returning student lounge with all kinds of notices about support group meetings for older students. Although Marilyn knew she would probably be among the oldest, she felt reassured that she would have some built-in support at the school.

What were Marilyn's *Strategies* for dealing with this? Could she balance work, school, and family demands as she made this change?

Marilyn was able to answer yes to all four questions. She is in an excellent place to think and plan seriously for this change. Her *Situation* was good. Her son was going to college, giving her the freedom to plan ahead. She was a risk-taker and considered herself resilient, so she rated her *Self* fairly high. Marilyn had some savings, but had also talked with the school and a bank to find out how to get a loan to cover her training. Her son was very encouraging, so her *Support* was in place. Having experienced some adversity in her life, she had learned to use various coping *Strategies* to help her, so her *Strategies* were high. She was clearly ready to retire and go for this career change.

LET'S RECAP

First, APPROACH your transition by identifying its type and indicating the degree to which it would alter your life. Second, TAKE STOCK by filling out Your 4 S Worksheet (see table 6.7). This will give you an assessment of where your strengths are and help you identify areas to work on.

Then TAKE CHARGE by developing your Action Plan (see table 6.8). You will visually see the resources that need help—your *Situation, Self, Supports,* and *Strategies.* You can then examine your list of possible coping *Strategies* and ask yourself the following series of questions:

- Should you take action to change the S's that are low? If so, which of the *Strategies* could you use?
- Should you try to change the way you see the S that needs help? If so, which of the *Strategies* seems most appropriate?
- Should you try to manage your reactions to the transition by reading, praying, jogging, or going into therapy?
- Or should you do nothing?

Again, remember that there may be other *Strategies* that you would find helpful that are not mentioned in this book. TAKING STOCK of your resources to cope with a particular transition or set of transitions is based on the assumption that your resources for coping—your four S's—are not static but will and can shift throughout your life.

TABLE 6.7.   YOU TAKE STOCK

APPROACHING CHANGE

- *Type:* _____
- *Impact on roles, relationships, routines, assumptions:* _____

TAKING STOCK OF YOUR COPING RESOURCES

Ratings	High	Okay	Low
• *Your Situation:* overall			
Your evaluation			
Timing			
Control			
Previous experience			
Other stress			
• *Your Self:* overall			
Response to transition (optimist, pessimist)			
Sense of well-being (mastery and pleasure)			
Self-knowledge			
• *Your Supports:* overall			
Getting affection, affirmation, aid			
Evaluation—getting enough and the right mixture			
Interrupted by transition			
• *Your Coping Strategies:* overall			
Taking action to change or modify your situation, supports, self, strategies			
Changing the way you see the transition			
Managing your reactions to transition			
Doing nothing			
Other			

TABLE 6.8. YOU TAKE CHARGE

Possible Coping Strategies   *Your 4 S's*

Taking Action to Change or Modify Your 4 S's
Negotiating
Taking optimistic action
Seeking advice
Asserting yourself
Brainstorming a new plan
Taking legal action
Other

Changing the Way You See Things
Applying knowledge of the transition process
Developing rituals
Making positive comparisons
Rearranging priorities
Reappraising, relabeling, reframing
Ignoring selectively
Denying
Engaging in humor
Having faith
Other

Managing Your Reactions to the Transition
Playing
Using relaxation skills
Expressing emotions
Engaging in physical activity
Participating in counseling, therapy, or support groups
Reading
Other
Doing Nothing
Using Other Strategies

Let me explain. After moving seventeen times, one woman said, "I have finally had it. No more." What had changed? Her husband, a career State Department official, had told her when they married to expect lots of moves. She did. They did. She saw herself as someone who could pick up, leave, and then dig in new roots. She was an optimist, used lots of coping *Strategies*, and was able to develop new *Supports* quickly. She was "high" on her four S's. But before the seventeenth move, she learned that she had cancer. She felt vulnerable and unable to just go and start over again. She did not feel she had the energy to make connections for herself and her young teenagers. In other words, her *Situation* had changed from high to low, influencing her evaluation of her ability to cope.

Someone else, another young woman who had been afraid to move, began to feel that she could move and travel. After several years of therapy, she realized that her fear had been based on anxiety about separating from everything familiar. She now realized her live-in partner would still be there for her, and her parents would still be there. In her case the biggest shift was in her *Self*.

Any of your four S's might, can, and will change. As they change, your ability to tackle transitions also changes. The encouraging aspect of this model is the knowledge that everything is not preordained. If you feel like a "loser," that can shift. If you feel you've got it together, that's great as long as you realize your *Situation*, *Self*, *Supports*, and *Strategies* might and can change.

Because your resources can and do shift, you can employ different *Strategies* to TAKE CHARGE, depending on which resources need strengthening.

As you can see, your coping resources are not precise or scientifically measurable, because to some degree they grow out of gut feelings and intuition. Don't be afraid to use these feelings along with the information from the chart to assess your *Situation*, your *Self*, your *Supports*, and your *Strategies*. With these tools you can determine where your vulnerabilities are; you can decide whether to move ahead and how.

These worksheets, your intuition, and your good sense are your guidelines for mastering change. Only you can decide whether and how to implement them. To encourage those who are feeling skeptical or overwhelmed, it is important to point out the creativity of those in transition who devise new ways to cope with and ultimately master and manage change.

7

TAKING CHARGE
OF YOUR NON-EVENT
TRANSITIONS

People often ask, "Am I alone in wondering what might have been?" No. In fact, these stories, in a sense, are everyone's stories. Each of these people has experienced that sense of what might have been, the earnest expectations that were not met, the dreams that somehow got lost along the way. It's true that some non-events might seem more significant than others, but who's to say? Does a thwarted beauty queen feel less pain than a childless man? And how might these adults deal with their pain and give new shape to the future?

We all experience what might have been, what should have been, what did not happen—what I call non-events. Yet, much research and counseling advice focuses on marker events like marriage, childbirth, changing jobs, divorce, and being fired. Most of these events are observable; many have rituals and celebrations attached to them. Paying attention to non-events—what they are, how they change lives, and ways they can be transformed—is important. A series of studies at the University of Maryland and a book Susan Robinson and I wrote titled *Going to Plan B: How You Can Cope, Regroup, and Start Your Life on a New Path* examined the extensiveness of non-events and how people can cope.[1] As a first step in the coping process it is important to

UNDERSTAND YOUR NON-EVENTS

The following stories provide a picture of how non-events impact lives.

"I gave up my career to stay home and raise my children, but they did not turn out as expected. I had a picture of them with sweaters tied around their shoulders and going to eastern colleges. Instead, one who had to go to a special school now works in a grocery store. Another dropped out of school and hasn't made a comeback. The third is a janitor. There is nothing wrong with them or what they are doing. I had spent my life expecting something different. I am so jealous when I read about other families where the children moved up and made something of themselves. Why do I walk around feeling depressed?"

"I always expected to be a parent. I love children, and feel I have a lot to give. My wife and I discovered we can never have children and my wife refuses to adopt. Am I going to spend the rest of my life angry at my wife and feeling cheated about not having children? I am really struggling with what to do now."

"My father never realized his dream of becoming a physician. Instead he sells pharmaceutical supplies and is a chronically unhappy individual. The problem is that his lost dream has affected our whole family, including my mother, my sister, myself. You wouldn't think someone else's lost dream would affect so many lives. We walk around him as if on eggshells. Is there a healthier way for our family to function?"

Where Do Unmet Dreams Reside?

We found that non-events occur in many areas: *relationships* that did not materialize; *family* problems such as infertility or not becoming a grandparent; *career* issues such as not getting a job, not being promoted, or missing an educational opportunity; and issues related to *Self* such as not shedding those extra pounds. In other words, people dream about love, family, success, legacy, and self-image.

Of course, life is not tidy—what starts out as a dream about career can impact dreams about self and family. The woman who discussed her father's career disappointment—not becoming a doctor—has influenced the family. His depression affected his wife. His disappointment in himself was projected onto his adult children. He expected them to perform, perform, and perform some more.

What Triggers Non-Events?

The triggers can be external, like a colleague getting promoted while you are still in the same job; others are internal, like some highly personal reminders that an expectation may never be realized. Whether internal or external, the underlying issue relates to feeling "off-time." Non-events are triggered when people feel that the events that they expected to occur in their lives should have already occurred and they are woefully behind. Despite what we know about variability in timing of transitions in adulthood, people still hold onto a picture of age-appropriate expectations.

Maria cried the night before her thirtieth birthday: "I don't give a damn about a career. I want a baby and family. It has not happened, and I am beginning to believe it is never going to happen. I don't want to celebrate my birthday." For several reasons, Maria has decided that her timetable has not been met. She is Hispanic with a family-oriented cultural heritage, and her sense of timing has triggered a feeling of great loss.

At the same time, another single woman Maria's age might be delighted that no family responsibilities interfere with a desire to advance her career. Clearly, what is a non-event and off-time for one person might be a desired state of affairs for someone else.

Four Types of Non-Events

Generally, four types of non-events can be identified: personal, ripple, resultant, and delayed.

Personal non-events refer to individual aspirations and might include not having a baby, not being promoted, or never marrying. For example, a person who has been in the same job for twenty years might present an example of nothing happening externally, yet everything has changed internally—that is, the person's assumptions about competency and identity have been gradually shaken. The expected job change never occurred, altering that person's assumptions about competency and identity.

Ripple non-events refer to the unfulfilled expectations of someone close to us, which in turn can alter our own *roles, relationships,* and *assumptions*. We interviewed the parents of two young adults who describe their children to friends as "just fine." Yet, they are upset because neither child has married. The parents are in their late sixties, and are not the grandparents or in-laws they expected to be. What is not happening to the adult children means that certain expected events are not happening to the parents. As we examine such disappointments more closely, we see that a non-event for one person may ripple significantly into another's life.

Resultant non-events start with an event that leads to a non-event. Take the example of the mother who gives birth to a child with multiple disabilities. From this traumatic event may come the resultant non-event of never being able to have another child. Or consider a rejection from medical school: The resultant non-event is failing to become a physician. The events themselves have a beginning and an end. Not being a physician can last a lifetime.

Delayed events are paradoxical. In our interviews, we found that adults keenly felt the loss of their dreams, the fear of never realizing a cherished expectation. Yet, they can be convinced that possibly their losses are merely delayed events. During the middle years, whenever they come, people begin to face the possibility that they are experiencing non-events, not delayed events. They begin to give up hope, and lose confidence that they can make the dream come true. The question of when an unrealized dream becomes a non-event rather than a delayed event is not clear-cut.

Are All Non-Events the Same?

Non-events differ in three critical ways: They can be hopeful or hopeless, sudden or gradual, in or out of one's control. The most crucial way in which they differ is in terms of the degree of hope surrounding these non-events. One man, a political exile, gave up all hope of ever returning to his country because of his political standing. And though his sadness remains, he has refused all offers of help. For him the situation is without remedy, and he is stuck in his private despair. Infertility, not having grandchildren, and rejection from a professional school are also viewed as hopeless. Absence of marriage, surprisingly, was not seen as hopeless. As long as there is breath, our respondents felt, there is a chance to meet the mate of one's dreams. Non-events perceived as hopeless will have the greatest impact on the adults who contend with them.

Some disappointments seem to broadside us suddenly. Ralph returned to college at age fifty, a hopeful turn after a sudden resultant non-event. He wrote on his non-event questionnaire: "I was groomed from childhood to some day run the family company. That was cut short when my father suddenly sold the business. After some agonizing, infuriating months, I have gone back to graduate school to study gerontology." Ralph faced a number of events: his father's sale of the business and his subsequent return to school. But what is often overlooked is the lost dream. Ralph wrote: "The non-event for me was that I had been groomed since childhood for a certain career. All my adult life, the company and its demands had been given first priority. This determined my relationship to friends, suppliers, employees, friends, wife, and family. My father's precipitously selling the business—a definite event—caused me to no longer have the role for which I had been prepared."

In a follow-up interview a year later, Ralph said, "When your pencil is broken you find out very rapidly who your real friends are. At home it was confusing to my children. I suddenly went from being the provider to a period of uncertainty and then, for want of anything better, I became a student. It was hard to suddenly have no office, no base. It also changed the way I saw myself. For years I had been the customer, not the vendor. I had no idea how difficult it is to sell oneself. But mostly I had expected to peak in my business career by age fifty. Instead, I am embarking on a new career. I am glad you are doing this study. Failure of a long-expected event to materialize can create more change in lifestyle, attitudes, social support than the occurrence of the event." Some non-events are out of our control, such as infertility or not having grandchildren. But even career and personal non-events can be beyond our power—no matter how hard we strive to avoid them. One woman told us: "In 1977, when I entered the Jesuit School of Theology at Berkeley, California, I thought I would be one of the first women to be ordained as a Roman Catholic priest. The papacy became more conservative; the U.S. bishops weakened, and repression of forward-thinking church people was rising. It was out of my control. It was part of the structure and system of the church. It's strange. I look the same to all my friends; I am doing the same thing I have always done, yet I feel so different. I am a perfect example of nothing happening but everything inside changing." We asked how this thwarting of her vocation changed her life. She used words like "betrayed," "angry," "powerless" to describe her initial feelings. Over time, she mobilized her anger and founded an organization helping women who feel oppressed. She also entered a Ph.D. program, preparing to become a therapist.

THE DREAM RESHAPING PROCESS

Coping with non-events requires reexamining your dreams. The basic issue is whether or not you hold on to them, modify them, or give them up. Each person goes through a process, not necessarily in the same order, not necessarily covering every part of the process. This is a process that takes time. People often ask, "How long will it take?" It would be great to provide a definitive answer, but the amount of time depends on the person, the particular non-event, and the supports one has.

Discovering

Since we usually do not acknowledge or talk about our non-events, the first step is to discover the non-event and give it a name. This has the double effect of diluting the power a non-event can have and of helping us take control of the situation. Strategies that give a non-event clarity include acknowledging it, labeling it, telling a story about it, and using metaphors to describe it.

When we first interviewed Betty, she said she thought the study was interesting, but it did not apply to her—she was in the midst of too many events, not non-events. She had just started a business, and she had two young children and a husband. Betty called back the next day asking for another interview. The realization had hit her: No, she had not experienced any non-events overnight, but she realized that her father's lost dream, his non-event, had significantly influenced her life. She felt he was pressuring her to be a superb wife and mother, while achieving great success in her business. Living with a depressed father and a disappointed mother had not been easy. Their non-events had rippled unhappily into her life. She said that just hearing the term "non-event" had greatly helped her become aware of what had been going on in their family. The awareness of the concept enabled her to articulate what her parents' problems were and how they influenced her.

Louis, who experienced a career non-event—he was passed over for promotion for seven years—did not know how to deal with this blow. Alternately, he felt anger, humiliation, even guilt that he should have performed better at work. His reactions were confusing and unsettling. Fortunately, he talked with his company's human resource person, who helped him take a reality check. He realized he was in a dead-end situation. He began talking about his career non-event and his emotional reactions to it. This enabled him to stop blaming himself and focus his energies on career planning. He also developed a story to tell his friends. His new mantra became "It's time for a change."

It is important to tell a story about the non-event; the story will then demystify the experience. The question of how to acknowledge your non-events to others is very important. People do not usually go around saying, "Let me tell you about my career non-event, or the job offer that never came." Unless you let others know you are experiencing a painful non-event, they will not know how to comfort you, or even that you need comforting. So telling a story, making your pain explicit, can also help mobilize others to mobilize you.

Grieving

People are expected to grieve over events like a death or rejoice over events like a promotion. But how do we help others to deal with their grief over what did not happen—a baby never conceived, a book never published, a relationship that never materialized? Grieving for non-events is difficult because the reason for the grief is unrecognized by others. Once the non-event or loss is acknowledged and named, then coming to terms with it can occur.

Kenneth J. Doka studies "disenfranchised grief"—a special kind of grief that is not recognized by society.[2] This is particularly applicable to non-events, since they are not public. There are no wakes, no chicken soup. The sadness is intensified: there is the loss of a loved one or dream and the loss of recognition from others. Labeling the grief and sharing it with others who are in a similar boat can be most helpful.

Some have started non-event support groups. For example, a support group for those sharing the loss of a dream can provide an opportunity for each person to state the particular lost dream and comfort others regarding their loss. It is easier to share with others experiencing similar pain—even if the lost dream is different—than to bury the emotions and try to go on. We need "good grief" before we can move on.

Refocusing

The next part of the process can be difficult because it requires letting go of old expectations and reframing the non-event. People often have difficulty changing their perceptions of themselves and the world and moving to a new vision. But shifting focus is necessary as we shape new goals by reframing our future selves and forcefully identifying a new dream, a new vision, or a new self.

We discussed the importance of rituals in the chapter on *Strategies*. But going back to Barbara Myerhoff's work shows their relevance for non-events. A major way to assist transformations is through the use of rituals. Myerhoff discussed the role of rituals, ceremonies, or rites of passage as a way to help people separate from the past and move into a new place. Rituals help people make sense out of the contradiction and paradox of many transitions—the paradox being that there is no single truth, there are many truths; that individuals are part of the past, but also the future. Myerhoff describes three stages of any ritual: First, the individual is segregated as in a graduation ceremony; second, the ritual acknowledges the somewhat bewildering phase in which the individual is between the old and the new; and third, the ritual helps the individual move into a new identity.[3]

Unfortunately, non-events are too often bereft of rituals. And non-events need rituals even more than events. Yet, developing them is a bit more difficult. However, an article in *Ms.* magazine helps us see the endless possibilities for developing non-event rituals. The following announcement says it all:[4]

> Alice and Carl Hesse
> are pleased to announce their daughter
> Susan A. Hesse
> is settling into
> joyous old maidhood
> after which she shall cease
> looking for Mr. Right
> and begin giving
> scintillating dinner parties and soirees.
> To help celebrate this wonderful occasion
> gift-place-settings
> are available at
> Macy's Department Store. . . . .

Ask yourself how you can develop a ritual for your non-event. First, name your non-event. Let's return to Janet, the eighteen-year-old who announced to her parents that she was not going to college, was moving out of their home and into an apartment with a roommate, and going to work as a waitress. The parents' non-event was their disappointment with their daughter's plans. Their expectation, based on their own experience, was that their daughter would be like all their friends' children and move from high school to college.

Part of their ritual was to identify their emotional reactions to the non-event. Example: They were embarrassed, disappointed, even angry. They then designed a ritual to help them grieve for the past that might never have been and move them closer to the future, keeping in mind that the ritual needs to be a shared activity with an opportunity for acknowledging and naming the past and rehearsing for the future. Example: To ease their pain, they invited another family (the daughters' godparents) over for a special dinner—a shared activity. They then made a speech to their daughter, giving her the money to install a phone but then saying she would have to pay the monthly bills. They also acknowledged her need to follow her own muse, stating that they would support any kind of future education or training when she was ready. Note: Their daughter eventually went to college, but the use of the ritual enabled the family to avoid the usual screaming fights that can attend such a decision. The ritual also helped the family define this transition as a positive, not a negative, transition.

Reshaping

Shifting focus is necessary as we shape new goals by reframing our future selves and forcefully identifying a new dream, a new vision, a new self. This includes taking stock, regaining control, and transforming the dream by imagining another more possible self.

As a small child David started playing the piano. At seven he was so talented that his music teacher had him do a solo performance. His mother, though not musical herself, made sure that he had lessons and instruments and went to musical events. At eleven David's life abruptly changed. His mother died, his father lost all his money because of the Depression, and his father and he moved from a large home to a boardinghouse in New York City. David was an only child. There was no time for music and life was quite a struggle. His father eventually became extremely successful and was one of the best-known labor arbitrators in the country. But during the Depression he borrowed heavily to keep them going and to send David away to boarding school. They selected one near New York so they could see each other.

Although they selected the school for proximity, it turned out to be the perfect school for David. It emphasized music and sports—his two loves. He played in the band, wrote songs, and was valedictorian of his class. By the time he graduated, his father was on the road back financially.

His father wanted him to go to Harvard; instead David selected Bard, which was then part of Columbia University. Bard was less traditional and had a strong music department. He met another musician there and together they started writing songs, trying to sell them, and had great plans for a future career together.

David pointed out how significant historical events were in shaping his life. When he graduated, World War II was in progress and he enlisted. During the next five years he concentrated on staying alive and never played a piano or engaged in music. At the end of the war, he married his present wife, whom he had met at college. They moved into a tiny place in New York—so tiny there was no room for a piano. However, he arranged to place his piano with a friend and he practiced daily at the friend's. He enrolled in a fine music school on the G.I. Bill, while his wife worked. His dream was to really move ahead in music. He felt that his wife supported this dream.

Once again external events—this time personal—interceded. He and his wife had decided not to have children until he finished his graduate work and was able to start supporting them. Very accidentally, his wife got pregnant. David began feeling tremendous pressure to move ahead with his career. He wrote to record companies in search of any kind of job in the music world. Letters went unanswered. He kept trying, but kept bumping into blind alleys.

Remembering the Depression, his father became frightened. He encouraged his son to move into the field of labor relations. David felt the pressure to move ahead and took a job in his father's field. At the time he did not realize the significance of his decision. He did not realize that his whole life would change course and he would never know if he could have really had a career that excited him, about which he was passionate. In our discussion, David said it would be too easy to blame the Depression, the war, the baby for his inability to move into music. He acknowledged all those forces but feels that maybe deep down he was afraid, afraid of failure. Statistically, very few make it in music. He wonders if he maybe did not have the "fire in the belly." He felt at the time he had no choice. As he looks back, he realizes he had a lot of choices.

For many years music played a significant role in his family life. At night there were music rituals to put their four children to bed; he played every night after work; and occasionally he talked to his old college buddy about trying to write songs professionally. Interestingly, three of his four sons entered the music field. David worries about them but is supportive of their dreams.

I asked David if he would agree that he reshaped his dream. He answered quickly, "I did not reshape my dream. I decided to go another way." Although he is successful by his and others' standards, he has a gnawing feeling that his life could have been different—more filled with passion and excitement with what he has loved since childhood.

David's case is instructive. What happened? How did David become a labor mediator/arbitrator rather than a musician? What forces shaped his life? How did the events and non-events in his life interact? What was his role in this decision? Was it in his control? Was it sudden? Has it led to despair?

David is able to look at his life and see the interplay of circumstances, history, and himself. He is also able to see the influence of events and non-events on his life. His is not a tragic story. It is a story of a man's life; it shows the importance of many factors in shaping one's life; it shows that any individual's life could have been lived many ways.

It is important to examine your lost dreams and make proactive decisions about what to do. Ask yourself, Is your non-event in your control? Is it time to let go and move on? Should you hold onto the dream and keep trying to make it? The dilemma is when to hold on to hope using new strategies or when to reshape the dream all together.

SPECIFIC STRATEGIES FOR COPING WITH NON-EVENTS

Coping with non-events may demand special strategies, since most non-events are hidden, most are losses, and there is usually no rehearsal for them. As you proceed with your own dream reshaping, you will need to assess which coping strategies to use. Richard Lazarus and Susan Folkman provide a means to organize your thinking.[5] They found that most strategies fall into one of two categories—problem-focused, which center on changing the source of the stress; and emotion-focused, which help people manage their feelings and change their thinking.

If you still have hope that your non-event is merely delayed, use problem-focused coping. For example, a young woman who had written a successful first novel spent a year trying to write her second one. She only wrote one chapter. She finally let go of that novel and is trying to think up another idea. But she has a Plan B if necessary—to return to magazine writing. However, she is not ready for Plan B. She is strategizing on ways to make her novel writing work out. She has several plans—to either go to a writer's retreat or join a writer's group.

If after several years she finds she cannot write the next book, she will go to emotion-focused coping. She will need to manage her emotions, grieve for her lost dream of becoming a novelist, and embrace Plan B, which still involves writing but not her original dream. All of us have scripts for our lives, some of which are interrupted and do not go according to plan. All of us have surprises—some positive, others negative. We cannot count on life just following a neat, arranged, linear script. Part of life is having alternative plans—from A through Z.

It is now time to go back to the 4 S System. As you deal with lost dreams that are lost forever, or ones that have a chance of becoming real you still need to garner all the resources you can. So, look at your *Situation*, *Supports*, *Self*, and coping *Strategies*. It is easy enough to plan on going to a writer's retreat, but what is your *Situation*? If you have an ill family member and no one to take over your caretaking role, your *Situation* is not good for going on a retreat. However, if you have strong substitute *Supports*, and if you can deal with any guilt feelings about leaving, maybe this is the time to go to the retreat. In other words, asses your resources, strengthen those that need it, and try to deal with your non-events.

AND IN CONCLUSION

Be aware that what looms as a lost dream for one person might not be an issue for someone else. In the long run, we are all looking for hope to outlast the broken dreams and for promise to ease the sorrow of defeat. By giving non-events their place in adult development, we can better understand that sometimes when nothing happens, everything changes.

YOUR NON-EVENT REVIEW

Name your non-event: _____

What type is it? Personal, ripple, resultant, or delayed? _____

_____

Do you feel hopeful that you can turn your non-event into an event?

If so, what problem-focused strategies will you use? _____

_____

If not, what emotion-focused strategies will you use? _____

_____

Will you go through the dream reshaping process of discovering, grieving, refocusing, reshaping? _____

_____

Rate your resources for coping:

Your *Situation*—Is it a strong resource? A weak resource?
Your *Supports*—Do you have good supports? Weak supports?
Your *Self*—Are you optimistic and resilient?
Your *Strategies*—Do you use lots of strategies?

8

TAKING CHARGE OF YOUR WORK/LIFE TRANSITIONS

The demands of work and personal life have always been regarded as two separate domains. Employees were expected to leave the personal side at home and concentrate on performing their job responsibilities efficiently and productively.

According to Stephanie Kay, human resource consultant, work/life balance has been the focus of many companies as managers realize that staff members are more productive when their individual needs are taken into account. In fact, many programs, such as flextime and day care, have been instituted to accommodate workers' personal lives. Kay wonders why so many employees suffer from an inability to integrate their work/life demands. "Why is there never enough time for family and personal needs? Why do so many people have demanding jobs only to climb ladders that lead nowhere or else to find the promised ladders no longer exist?"[1] Sociologist Phyllis Moen and psychologist Patricia Roehling explain the "mismatch" of the career dream and the economic and workplace realities in their book *The Career Mystique*,[2] underscoring the obvious fact that most employees have family responsibilities but that the model of the husband going off to work with the helpmate handling home and family no longer exists.

The world has changed. Families exist in many forms: single parents, same sex parents, stay-at-home fathers, and grandparents raising grandchildren. Everyone is stressed; no one has the amount of time and support necessary to negotiate work/family transitions. At first, I was going to write two separate chapters—one on work transitions and the other on family transitions. However, they are so intertwined that it is impossible to treat them apart. This chapter is organized in two sections. The first will present a number of vignettes of people handling the complexity of work/life; the second section will look at underlying issues as people move in, through, and out of work/family life.

HANDLING WORK AND FAMILY: SOME CASES

Combining work and family—a growing necessity today—is not an either-or situation. Many couples simultaneously report strain and benefits. One working mother asked her daughter if she should feel guilty about working. Her daughter's reply: "You are so involved with us as it is, I can't imagine what it would have been like if you had been home full-time." However, others report ambivalence as they work to moderate the demands of work and family.

The ambivalence is both sociological and psychological. Sociological ambivalence refers to the conflicting norms inherent in a role. For example, there are "structural dilemmas"—those that are inherent in the relationship between the conflicting needs of one's family and one's workplace. This can be seen when talking with women, and more and more with men, who are torn between the demands of work and family. At thirty-nine, Colleen had her first baby, after trying for several years. Since she was the main breadwinner, she was forced to go back to work—her health insurance was significantly better than her husband's. She would have been thrilled to be a stay-at-home mom; she had a talent with babies. The day she returned to work after a six-month leave of absence (only one month of it was paid leave), she cried all the way to work.

Psychological ambivalence refers to two or more opposing emotions. An example: Megan loved her father; Megan resented her father. She admired him, she was deeply connected to him, but she resented his subtle desire to control her. She was dependent on him for financial help, making it all the more difficult to break away. Or take Jim, whose mother lived with him. He cared about her, even thought he loved her, yet resented her for being a burden, for restricting his activities and his freedom. Of course, he was also angry at himself for allowing this to happen.

Other poignant examples include the millions of grandparents raising grandchildren, often because their adult children are dead, incarcerated, or on drugs. As Rose said, "I would not have it any other way. My grandson needs me and I will always be there for him. But my anger at my son for his irresponsible behavior sometimes gets out of control."

We could point out example after example of family relationships filled with ambivalence—the societal demands on people to care for and support their families; the psychological feelings of happiness to be able to give back to one's family; the conflicting emotions of feeling that one has been cheated or burdened.

Again, this all underscores the importance of addressing issues of work and family.

Alan Changes His Situation

Many, like Alan, cannot separate work and family. As we will see, Alan's moods and depression at work spilled over into his family life. I asked: "As a son, father, husband, and involved career person how do you balance these? Where are the pressures that exhaust you? Describe a time when you felt a little unhinged by all these pressures."

Alan's answer:

"As a son, father, husband, and career person, I would say that my ability to balance these is a bit worse than many people. I do not deal with the pressure well. What people say is true—you do what you have to do in order to survive. For me personally, my home life tends to suffer as a result of my emotional investment in my work life. The scales are not even.

"The pressures that exhaust me most are far and away the husband/father portions of my life. For many reasons, I find that it is my home life that causes 85 percent to 90 percent of my stress. I want to be a good father, a positive role model, a dependable figure, a loving leader. I want to be a responsible husband, a good lover, a reliable friend and partner. I fear that I am not reaching my goals in those areas.

"One of the worst periods in my life, as it relates to feeling the pressures of my various 'identities,' was when we had the mold crisis in our home. I felt as though my family was in serious trouble—our health was compromised—and we had very limited resources (financially mostly) to do anything about it. What went through my mind during that entire time was if I were a better father/husband, I'd be a better person."

Alan TAKES STOCK

Alan felt he was shortchanging his family and felt miserable at work. He saw his *Situation* as low. On the positive side, his *Supports* were strong. He asked for and received support from his mother and wife. In fact, his mother offered to give him funds to attend a workshop designed to uncover new options. He saw himself as both negative and positive. Although he tends to catastrophize, he knows he is creative and will develop new options. At the time of the interview, he was not using all the *Strategies* at his disposal.

Alan TAKES CHARGE

Alan knew he needed to change his *Situation*. He talked with a career counselor who told him of an institute in California where he could explore his life goals and develop strategies to implement them. He took a leave from his job, went to California with his mother's financial support, and discovered what he wanted to do. He came back energized. With his wife's emotional support, he resigned from the job he did not like. It took him three nerve-wracking months, but he finally got just the job he wanted. His new job has been wonderful.

So, by relying on his *Supports* and his creativity, and using new *Strategies* that he learned at the institute, he was able to change his *Situation*. In a recent follow-up interview, I saw a very productive, fulfilled person. He is still working to strengthen himself by meeting with a therapist. He wants to control his depression so that it does not spill over into both family and work.

When Health Changes Everything—Fred

Fred was overwhelmed. He retired as a pharmacist at age seventy-seven. After retiring, he placed his wife, Bessie, in a nursing home, at the urging of his children.

His story was a simple one. He married his sweetheart. They worked together in their own drugstore until he was shot. After that, they worried about their safety and at age sixty moved to Florida where he passed his boards so he could continue working as a pharmacist. This worked out well until Bessie had a stroke. He was her caregiver, and did this out of love, not guilt or necessity. During this time, he hurt his back, and he now walks hunched over with a cane. Despite three epidural shots he is in constant pain. Gradually, Bessie developed Alzheimer's disease. Fred thought that if he retired he could care for her more fully. But her condition deteriorated rapidly and Bessie is now in a nursing home.

Fred is lost and vulnerable. He will not leave their house because he holds onto the dream that he will get strong enough to bring Bessie home, even though his children are trying to tell him that won't happen. He is not ready to give up the dream.

Let's look at Fred's 4 S's: His *Situation* is negative and overwhelming but his *Supports* are over the top. His daughter adores him, supports him, and relies on his judgment. She recently consulted him about a job choice she had. He encouraged her to take the risky course because that is what she wanted to do. She encouraged him to take care of himself, to get out of the house, and to move ahead with his volunteer activities. His view of *Self* is a bit shaky, but he clearly has signs of resiliency. And he is beginning to expand his coping *Strategies*.

Even though Fred has experienced the bottom dropping out of his world, and he sees his world as out of his control, he is still slowly inching forward. He has figured out what he can do in retirement. Of course, the main event will be his visits to Bessie, at least three times a week. But he has wisely decided to get certified as a diabetic counselor and has offered to volunteer at the local hospital. He was known as an excellent pharmacist so they are pleased that he will be on board.

Helen Changes Her Self-Image

Let's look at the experience of Helen, a building engineer, whose primary work responsibilities involved fixing leaks in a building, checking out electrical problems, confirming that the heat and air conditioning were working properly, and being on call to address any emergencies.

She took the first job several years ago, in an office building, and after six months she left it. In order to understand what happened, let's TAKE STOCK of Helen's 4 S's. At the time she took the job she was in a trying *Situation*. She had just left her husband and had total responsibility for three small children. The combination of job and personal changes was very stressful. Helen began to blame herself for not being able to make a go of her marriage and began thinking globally about her *Self* as a failure. She had some *Supports* among family members, but at work there was little support and little control over what she did. She punched a clock and followed the rules, but never was told she was doing a good job. She spent most of the time in the boiler room and had little contact with anyone at work. Helen's greatest resource was her willingness to try many *Strategies* at home and at work. Overall she had three "low" S's and one "high" S.

More recently, Helen took a similar job in another office building. She is now living with a man who is very involved with her children and very committed to her well-being. She sees her *Situation* as excellent. Although she still tends to downplay her own capabilities, Helen is now aware of her tendencies to see the glass as half empty rather than half full. Her *Support* at home and work is now "high." Her boss at work is very appreciative of her performance and keeps saying how lucky he is to have her on his staff. Her coping *Strategies* are good; she is able to be assertive when necessary, to hold back when appropriate, and to think differently at times.

Work-related transitions, whether we are employed or unemployed, have certain characteristics and phases in common. Yet, as Helen's story shows, what we bring to the transition at a particular time of life may determine to a large extent whether we master it. TAKING STOCK of your 4 S's will enable you to identify the areas you need to bolster to help you cope with the transition: your *Situation*, your *Self*, your *Supports*, or your *Strategies*.

CHAPTER 8

Monique Utilizes Multiple Strategies

As I listened to Monique's *Situation*, I kept wondering how she was coping, what she would and could do. Her *Situation* was negative. She had a three-year-old and a four-month-old without a husband or financial stability. She had a job so she felt she could take care of herself. However, the day she was to return to work after having her second child, she learned that her job had been eliminated. She was overwhelmed: Her *Situation* was negative and she had left her major *Support*.

She decided that she needed to increase her *Supports*. She has good friends and a good professional network where she currently lives. However, she decided to move nearer her sister and brother-in-law until she gets her bearings. She knows she can temporarily lean on her sister in a way that she cannot with friends. "I need to free fall and have someone catch me."

Monique is concerned about making professional contacts since she will have to start all over again. She is trading friends and a familiar community to be with family. In addition, her about-to-be ex-husband has moved to the town where she will be moving so he can stay involved with the children. She is pleased that he has been able to control his addictions and get employment. That money will help her. She is right now grieving for the friends and life she has known and is leaving.

Monique has always seen her *Self* as very sufficient and someone who could always accomplish what she had in mind. She now realizes that her life is not perfect and that she has to let go of the unrealistic standards she has set for herself. "I can only do my best."

In addition, she has had a real shift in the way she sees herself. She realized she was a codependent, enabling her husband's addictions. Once she realized her part in this, she was able to have what she called "a paradigm shift in the way I see myself." This realization pushed her to decide once and for all the marriage was over.

She labels herself resilient, optimistic, and brave. Her resilience is obvious as she learns to go with the flow instead of planning everything. Her optimism was evident when she claimed, "I know next year will be a good year." Her attitude will play a key role in her survival. She is brave as she leaves everything she has known and moves into the unknown.

Monique used *Strategies* to *change the meaning* of her multiple transitions. During her newborn son's stay in the hospital she turned to God and looked to a higher power. She recognized that life was somehow unmanageable, and turning to God enabled her to "detach" from her husband. Her belief system began to work and now it is a habit. "Instead of trying to manage my husband I began to let go, to pray, to detach. It worked."

She also started employing strategies that would *change her Situation* by creating a website and taking on private clients. This extra money could help her get on top again. She is also beginning to consider ways to earn money when she moves to a new community.

She tries to *manage her reactions* by using relaxation techniques, writing in a diary, talking with a counselor, and joining a support group.

All in all, Monique is facing her future embracing the ambiguity of what's next instead of fighting it.

John's Move to Gain Control

John is a young man who was in a partnership with two others in restoring an old farm that they hoped to sell. The partners began to disagree about how much each was doing. They began to think of dissolving the partnership. However, John argued that he had already invested a considerable amount of time and money in the project and had given up other work opportunities. How could he regain control?

John found that he could APPROACH this work transition as a learning experience and that it was not necessary to make a long-term commitment to it. This helped him view the experience as important for "learning the ropes" about restoration and about working in a partnership, and for understanding more about business. As he TOOK STOCK of his resources for dealing with the partner disagreement, he realized that his *Situation* was excellent. He had decided to enter this partnership to see if he wanted to become a contractor and restorer. At the same time he had other pressures: he was in school and he had a very low income. Despite these negatives, he appraised his *Situation* as good. His *Supports* were good. He had a live-in partner who would listen sympathetically as he recounted his aggravations and would actually help him at the property. In addition, his father knew a good deal about partnerships. In general, he felt pretty good about his *Self.*

But John's *Strategies* for coping with new situations were limited. He often whined and complained and acted as if he could not control things that happened to him. To TAKE CHARGE, he realized that he needed to increase the number of *Strategies* he used. To do this, he asked himself, "Should I change them, think about them differently, manage my reactions to stress, or take no action?" John knew he needed to move from taking no action to taking action, learning to negotiate and assert himself. He actually TOOK CHARGE by suggesting that they dissolve the partnership. No one wanted that, so he started negotiations about different ways to work together that would be mutually beneficial. The problem is not resolved yet, but John feels as if he is doing something, not just complaining.

Amy Handles Her Overwhelming Schedule

Amy felt totally overwhelmed. She said, "I get very overwhelmed with work and dealing with my three young children. I separated when my kids were one, six, and nine. Once the divorce was final, I decided to forge fast ahead—putting my house on the market, looking for a new neighborhood with good public schools.

"I tried to figure out what I could do to make money, be available to my kids, and keep my sanity. I decided on becoming a personal trainer. I signed up for the certification class, passed the exam, and spread the word. Within two years my schedule was filled.

"I wake up every day at 4:20 a.m. and am out my door by 5:30 a.m. My day is not over until 5 p.m. I come home beyond exhausted and all three kids run out to my car and start talking—yelling—at me at once. I deal with fighting, homework, screaming, and complete insanity when all I want to do is rest on the sofa because I am so exhausted.

"Looking at the 4 S System can explain why I am surviving this in good shape. My *Situation* is stressful but I use lots of coping *Strategies*. First, I am very organized. I have two calendars, make lists, pack my lunch at night, and arrange the children's schedule the night before. I also talk to myself, telling myself that in a few hours things will settle down and I can start unwinding and get ready for bed. I try to plan a fun activity for myself on the weekends I do not have the kids. In addition I plan dinner with a friend every Wednesday night when my husband takes the kids. When I feel panicky about my work schedule, I tell myself to focus on one hour at a time.

"In addition to *Strategies*, I have wonderful support from my Mother and friends. They are there for me, and sometimes if a child gets sick my Mother will baby-sit. Actually, I feel very lucky. I am out of a bad marriage, am caring for my kids and myself. But it is overwhelming sometimes."

To Conclude

There are many other instances of work/family conflicts and spillover. For example, the millions of grandparents raising grandchildren, single parents returning to school, or parents in two jobs with children arguing about who should take the day off when a child is ill. The cases are endless and each is idiosyncratic. But once again, the BIG question is what to do about it?

WORK/LIFE TRANSITIONS: MOVING IN, THROUGH, AND OUT

I assume that if everyone had a better understanding of work transitions, this could reduce stress and provide relief on the home front.

Work is a core experience in the life of almost every adult. Its undeniable importance is demonstrated by the fact that most of us spend about half our waking hours for the major part of our lives engaged in work. But work is too significant to be defined only in terms of the time spent on it, because where we work, the type of work we do, what we get paid for it, how we relate to other workers, and work's impact on our personal and family lives all play a major role in defining our role in society. Work, in all its facets, dominates a major part of the life of most people.

Furthermore, the pace of technological change has turned the workplace and our work/family lives into a hotbed of transitions. Moen and Roehling described these: "Together, couples choose jobs, homes, parenthood, work hours, leisure, geographical moves, and commutes. . . . One spouse's opportunities and constraints invariably affect the choices and options of others."[3]

Your approach to change will be easier once you have a basic understanding of the transition process. Every transition does not alter your life in the same way. Some are big and alter all aspects of your life; others only change one aspect. Furthermore, transitions do not occur at only one point in time. Rather, each one is a process that reveals itself over time. Your reactions and emotions change from the beginning of that process to the time when you finally integrate the change into your life.

This knowledge can help you in two ways. First, just knowing that today is not forever, that your reactions will change over time, and that only you know if a transition is a major one, can be a comfort. However, you will see that you need different kinds of support and help, depending on where you are in the transition process. Let's play this out for work/family transitions and see if this knowledge can help you approach your next work transition more effectively.

If we look at work transitions as processes over time, we can place them in one of three categories: moving in, moving through, and moving out. Your reactions as you move into a new job or a new family situation will differ from your reactions as you move through or out. In addition, the strategies you employ to smooth the transitions will differ depending on whether you are moving in, through, or out.

Moving In: "Learning the Ropes"

Whenever you take a new job, whether it is a first job, a new job at the same level, or a promotion, you need to "learn the ropes." One man reported his confusion when on the first day of his job as administrative assistant his boss announced that "we have several meetings today." When the boss got ready to go to the first meeting, the administrative assistant also prepared to attend. The boss quickly explained that the assistant was not to join him. In this case the new employee needed to get used to the language of the boss—that *we* really meant him, not the assistant.

In a similar case, the new vice president of a company was unaware of the informal expectation that all executives would eat in the executive dining room at a particular time. She kept making lunch dates with people she knew in other organizations. Some time passed before she realized that her lack of knowledge about the informal norms had been responsible for her being excluded from the inner circle. In another case a man reported his surprise when he learned the unwritten rule that he was expected to raise money to support his salary and his office—a matter that had never been mentioned during the job interviews and orientation. And most recently, I received a letter from a woman executive who had tracked her first day on a temporary assignment with an agency. She wrote:

"I felt a little like a schoolgirl going back to school after a summer vacation. I felt excited about the possibilities. I knew what to expect in general, but the specifics of a new class, and a new teacher were unknown. When I arrived, there was no formal welcoming but I have had enough jobs to know how to take care of myself. I quickly identified the person who could be the biggest help, the secretary to the head of the department. By allying with her, I realized that I would learn the rules and procedures. She made me feel at home."

Meryl Louis, an organizational specialist, suggested that all newcomers to the workplace are in for a surprise about what is expected and, furthermore, that turnover and stress occur because of unrealistic, inflated, and unmet expectations.[4] Your transition can be eased, however, when you realize that *any* new situation will probably evoke feelings of uncertainty and that each time you move into a new setting you will need to learn the ropes. Then you can seek help from an "informal socializing agent," a colleague who can help you understand the procedures and expectations in your new employment; an individual experienced in the transition you are about to undertake. Just knowing that adjusting to transitions takes time and that your reactions will change as you are in the new work or family role will be some comfort.

We can apply the same principles to family and personal transitions. For example, the process of falling "in lust," to falling in love, to forming a permanent bond is complex. At first, you need to learn the ropes. What does it mean to be committed? How do you behave? What is expected of you? And then for those who have a child, the adjustment to this entirely new situation can be overwhelming.

Jan and Al went through the stages of falling in lust and in love, to marriage. They were joined at the hip. Even buying gift wrapping involved togetherness, whether choosing the color of the paper, or deciding to wrap the gift or put it in a gift bag. Then, their planned-for baby arrived. Jan became besotted by the baby. At first, Al was involved. But after a few months he began feeling left out. Over time he became jealous of the baby. Al and Jan began fighting and falling out of lust and love.

As *Newsweek* reporter Lauren Picker reported, "Research shows that marriage takes a hit when baby makes three. Generation X parents in particular are reeling. According to a 2003 analysis of 90 studies involving 31,000 married people, the drop in marital satisfaction after the first baby's birth is a staggering 42 percent larger among the current generation of parents than their predecessors."[5]

Of course, there are many instances of mutual joy. But whether the new family situation results in joy, confusion, or upset, introducing a new person into the equation takes time and requires "learning the ropes."

The same can be said for any life transition—divorce, returning to school, or even retiring. We often have no ready role models to tell us how to behave. As one widowed, retired woman said to me, "I am dating three men. What if one of them makes a move on me? What do I do?"

Getting through this initial period is less trying if you can get some extra doses of support. Some techniques include informational interviews with people in fields of interest. Such encounters can lead to informal mentoring, brainstorming, or counseling. I often suggest that those looking for work consider volunteering one day a week with a person or organization that is relevant to their interests. By making yourself invaluable, you might create a job for yourself. It is also helpful to connect with others in your same family situation. There are many support groups for first-time mothers, newly divorced, grandparents raising grandchildren. It helps to realize that you are not alone.

Moving Through

If the motto for those moving in is "learn the ropes," the motto for those moving *through* could be "hang in there, baby!" After working in the same job for some time, many of us begin to lose enthusiasm for it, especially if we feel stuck and see no possibility of change or promotion. This can result in burnout.

Many have pointed to marriage burnout. John Gottman, marriage researcher and director of the Relationship Research Institute in Seattle, studies couples who remain happy. He offers suggestions for how to reduce burnout and keep romance alive. He can also predict which couples will make it in the long run.

The increase in midlife divorces indicates marriage burnout. The majority of midlife divorces are initiated by women. Women felt free at last and found the newfound independence rewarding. Men were upset by the split, fearing loss of contact with their children. In fact, a story in the *New York Times*, "Middle-Aged Men Find that It's Cold on Mars," quoted a number of men who had been blindsided by the divorce and felt lonely. One man exclaimed that the unwanted breakup would postpone his wanted retirement.[6]

Judith Bardwick suggested that bored employees confront three types of plateaus: structural, content, and life. *Structural* plateaus occur when an employee has no place to go in the organization itself, no new job possibilities, because of the structure of the organization. As an example, Bardwick described IBM, which at that time employed 383,000 employees, 44,000 managers, 6,000 middle managers, 1,400 executives, and 50 core leaders.[7] Clearly, only a very small proportion of employees could continue to move up.

Of course, not everyone wants to move up. Many people are challenged by the work at hand, while others are unhappy doing the same work. I asked a clerical worker what she would do if there were no obstacles, and she answered, "Just what I am doing." Yet, many clerical workers feel they are plateaued. In fact, clerical work is seen as a highly stressful occupation with high demand and low control. That is, workers are under enormous pressure and have little control over what they do and when.

However, many workers are bored because of job content; they have been doing the same job for a number of years. They know what to expect every day. The value of sabbaticals—academics' chance to get away and retool—has been recognized by several other professions. But most professionals and blue-collar workers don't have the luxury of taking a breather. For those who have some discretionary time in their jobs, boredom can be alleviated by assigning new activities while retaining the same jobs. For example, one employee had been doing the same job for fifteen years. She found out that her company had a tuition reimbursement plan and she entered a graduate program in counseling. As a result of taking courses, she instituted a planning seminar for the firm's employees who were considering retirement. This added a new twist to what the organization regularly did. This enterprising employee had the same job and the same title but was engaging in new activities that energized her.

If you are fortunate enough to work in an organization that has a policy that encourages worker participation, you are less likely to be bored. According to many studies, workers consulted about how to improve their jobs and how to work cooperatively become more involved and productive. Unfortunately, most people don't work in such forward-thinking organizations and need to redesign their jobs in other ways. One domestic worker does this by only accepting jobs in homes where she is encouraged to clean the house as she thinks best. She reports that many employers want to tell her what to do and when. She is good at her work and will not work in homes where all control is taken from her.

A midlife man, Jules, working as an engineer, fits into what Bardwick labels *a life plateau.*

"I just got this feeling that I'm kind of just dead-end. I got a job, it's all right, but there is no future. And I see younger men getting ahead of me. Here I have a house, a mortgage. I don't have the free-dom to move as they do, but yet I get passed over for promotions. I got a good job, but it is going nowhere; it's just absolutely becoming part of my life that I don't like. I come to work, I do my job, I go home—there's no challenge. . . . . If only I saw someplace I could move, someplace I could go, someplace I could get ahead, do some of the things I really wanted to do when I started in this organization. . . . The kids are getting older, I'm becoming less necessary there. You look at this organization—I'm becoming less necessary here. I've got a lot to offer. I just don't know what to do with it."

Jules, bored with life, was experiencing a non-event. His daily rou-tines were not changing, but something more basic *was* changing—the way he saw himself. He was seeing himself as a loser, as non-essential, as a person with no future. His roles and relationships changed when an employee who had previously worked for him became his supervisor. Many plateaued employees are experiencing non-events, but they lack the support that comes when transitions are more observable.

Jules felt that he was a fairly good coper, that he used lots of *Strategies*, and that he had good *Supports* at home. What he wanted to change was his *Situation*. He had several choices: talk with his boss and suggest a brainstorming session about how he could be more use-ful to the company; join a support group at his church called "So you're having a mid-life crisis"; or seek career counseling and think systematically about what he really wanted to do with the rest of his life. If he did not want to take direct action, another possible approach would be to try to change the meaning of his work situa-tion by telling himself that work is only one part of life and directly focusing more on strengthening his life outside work. He could also choose to manage his reactions to his work by relaxation or by putting everything on hold and doing nothing. In other words, he has lots of choices about how to take charge of his *Situation*.

Moving Out

Molly, a Peace Corps retiree, enrolled in my class on transitions, hoping that it would help her better understand and handle her own transition. As a volunteer she received extensive orientation, both to the country she would work in and to the overall norms and expectations of the Peace Corps. During her tenure she had had support from other volunteers and had never felt burned out. But leaving made her feel purposeless and depressed. The contrast of going from an environment in which she had felt she really mattered, was appreciated, and was noticed to one in which she was just an individual left her feeling "rudderless." She had no help in coping with this leaving process and was confused about how to proceed.

The process of writing a paper about a proposed workshop for retiring Peace Corps volunteers was therapeutic for her and others. In fact, the Peace Corps is now offering a program to assist volunteers as they leave the corps and reenter their lives back home.

Meryl Louis compares the "leave-taking process . . . to closing out ledger books account by account, but without knowing until the process is actually occurring what the titles of the accounts . . . will be."[8]

Whether you are fired or leave a job for a promotion, there is bound to be disruption in your life. One woman who voluntarily left one college presidency for another said, "My biggest surprise was depression. I had loved being at my former institution, but felt it was time to leave. I accepted a job at a more complex institution and was very excited about the new job. I expected sadness about leaving so many friends and colleagues. What I did not expect was the pain to continue. I have been gone for six months, and I still cry easily."

College graduates, whose "work" for years has been studying, may experience some of the same problems of moving out as those leaving the workforce. For many, there is an inevitable letdown until a new sense of purpose can be articulated. The learners moving out are giving up classes, advisers, and the goal of "becoming," but they may not have a clear vision of new goals. Change involves loss as well as gain. Grief often accompanies leaving one set of activities, even when the change is desired. There are contradictory impulses—a yearning for the past and a drive to formulate new agendas.

TO SUMMARIZE

All through life you will undergo many work and family transitions. You will move into many new situations that require you to "learn the ropes." You will also find yourself remaining in job or family situations where you need to develop strategies that will enable you to "hang in there." Many times you will leave a job where your task is to "let go and reinvest." There will also be times when you are trying to get in or out of a relationship, where you need help to "stay the course."

Recognizing that work/family transitions are characterized by different needs as we move in, through, and out, we can apply the steps previously outlined in this book to master these changes. The key elements in achieving this mastery are APPROACHING CHANGE by understanding the transition process; TAKING STOCK of our resources for coping; and TAKING CHARGE by strengthening those resources.

YOUR WORK/LIFE REVIEW

Some Questions to Consider

Name your major issue: _____
Does it stem from work?   Yes   No
Does it stem from family?   Yes   No
What can you do about it? How can you bring balance to your
    work/life?

9

IT'S YOUR TURN NOW

Your approach to change will be easier once you have a basic understanding of transitions and their impact on your life. Every transition does not affect your life in the same way. Some are big and alter
all aspects of your life; others only change one aspect. Furthermore,
transitions do not occur at only one point in time. Your reactions and
emotions change from the beginning of that process to the time when
you finally integrate the change into your life.

This knowledge can help you in two ways. First, just knowing
that today is not forever, and that your reactions will change over
time, can ease the pain associated with change. Second, you will find
that you need different kinds of support and help depending on
where you are in the transition process.

In order to make this structure concrete and one that you can apply
to your situation, Stephanie Kay and I developed a Transition Guide
and Questionnaire.[1] The Guide is included in the book so that you can
apply everything we have covered to your particular transition. To help
you fill out the Guide, review your answers to the exercises at the end of

most chapters. Although you are filling out the Guide around one transition, you can use it as a way to develop an action plan for future transitions.

So now it is your turn. Fill out the Guide and develop your own action plan.

THE TRANSITION GUIDE AND QUESTIONNAIRE

A New Way to Think About Change

The Transition Guide (TG) can help you think about your own change. The Guide includes a questionnaire, a summary of your scores, a brief description of the transition model, and some discussion questions.

By completing the self-scoring TG, you will find ways to increase your readiness for change—whether it is change you have initiated or change that has happened to you. The TG will enable you to take stock of your resources for coping with change, which include your

- *Situation*—What is going on in your life at the time of change;
- *Self*—Your internal resources for dealing with change;
- *Supports*—The people and activities you can count on for support during your transition; and
- *Strategies*—Your ability to use a variety of coping strategies.

Coping with transitions involves counting your resources—your *Situation*, your *Self*, your *Supports*, and your *Strategies*. Filling out this questionnaire will give you a measure of these resources. It will identify areas from which you can draw strength as well as areas you must focus on to cope successfully. In the sections on the following pages, please answer each question as it relates to the transition you have in mind (see table 9.1). This questionnaire will produce more useful insights if you think of a specific transition, rather than transitions in general.

You will receive a score for each of your resources. Your scores will be presented in a way so that you can easily see which resources will serve as your strengths and which will need bolstering. You can then take charge of your transition by developing an action plan that takes account of your strengths.

The TG gives you new ways to creatively take charge of change. It will help you gain a greater sense of personal control over all types of transitions.

TABLE 9.1.   NAME YOUR TRANSITION

_____

Where are you in this transition?
_____ Beginning _____ Middle _____ End

Situation_____

How You See It
Situation is the overall picture surrounding a transition. Circle the number that best describes your situation on each of the following items.

1. Looking ahead, I feel able to
   Plan ahead with great difficulty   Plan ahead with great ease
       1   2   3   4   5

2. For me, this situation is happening at the
   Worst possible moment   Best possible moment
       1   2   3   4   5

3. I see my situation as
   Totally out of personal control   Totally within personal control
       1   2   3   4   5

(continued)

TABLE 9.1.   (CONTINUED)

4. This transition will be likely to cause

Much stress in other roles in my life			Little stress in other roles in my life	
1	2	3	4	5

5. I view this situation as

Totally undesirable				Totally desirable
1	2	3	4	5

6. From where I stand now, this situation is likely to be of

Unmanageable duration			Manageable duration	
1	2	3	4	5

7. I expect to bring to this transition

No benefit of previous experience			Great benefit of previous experience	
1	2	3	4	5

8. The outcome of the transition is likely to be

Extremely negative				Extremely positive
1	2	3	4	5

9. I am currently dealing with other stressors in my life

Much concurrent stress			Little concurrent stress	
1	2	3	4	5

10. In my culture this transition would

Not be accepted				Be easily accepted
1	2	3	4	5

Add the numbers you have circled for items 1–10, and write the sum here:_____.

Self_____

Who You Are

Self is the inner strength that you bring to a transition. Circle the number that best describes your position on each of the following items.

11. I feel a sense of control or mastery as I face transitions

Never   Always

1   2   3   4   5

12. I usually face life as

A pessimist   An Optimist

1   2   3   4   5

13. When I think about how resilient I am in the face of change, I would describe myself as

Not very resilient   Extremely resilient

1   2   3   4   5

14. I feel that I really understand myself

Not well at all   Extremely well

1   2   3   4   5

15. In responding to this transition, I find myself with

Not enough physical or   Ample physical or
emotional energy   emotional energy

1   2   3   4   5

16. This transition is in line with my values (i.e., what is important to me)

Not at all   Completely

1   2   3   4   5

17. When things go wrong, I blame myself

Usually   Rarely

1   2   3   4   5

18. I feel good about myself

Rarely   Mostly

1   2   3   4   5

19. I know how to meet my needs when going through transitions

Seldom   Always

1   2   3   4   5

20. My expectations are realistic

Seldom   Mostly

1   2   3   4   5

(continued)

TABLE 9.1. (CONTINUED)

Add the numbers you have circled for items 11–20, and write the sum here:_____.

Supports_____

What Help You Have from Others

Supports are the external resources available to deal with change. Circle the number that best describes the supports available to you in each of the following items.

As I anticipate or experience this transition, can I count on support from:

21. My family?
    Inadequate Support   Fully Adequate Support
         1   2   3   4   5

22. My spouse or partner?
    Inadequate Support   Fully Adequate Support
         1   2   3   4   5

23. My friends?
    Inadequate Support   Fully Adequate Support
         1   2   3   4   5

24. A group, other than my family or friends? (i.e., co-workers, support groups, or other professional group)
    Inadequate Support   Fully Adequate Support
         1   2   3   4   5

We need various types of support at different times. Circle the number that best describes the kind of support you are getting or anticipating getting during this transition.

25. Affection
    Needs unmet   Needs fully met
         1   2   3   4   5

26. Respect for the way I'm handling this transition

Little respect			High degree of respect	
1	2	3	4	5

27. Assistance

Little help				Much help
1	2	3	4	5

28. Feedback (reality check)

Little				Much
1	2	3	4	5

29. I have a variety of support activities (intellectual pursuits, hobbies, athletics, volunteerism, etc.)

Few				Many
1	2	3	4	5

Add the numbers you have circled for items 21–29, and write the sum here:_____.

Strategies_____

How You Cope

Strategies are actions taken to cope with a transition. How effective are you at using these skills? Circle the number which best describes your effectiveness in each of the following skill areas:

1 = Very Ineffective   2 = Ineffective   3 = Average   4 = Effective
5 = Very Effective

30. Negotiating (compromising, talking things through)

	1	2	3	4	5

31. Taking action (mobilizing yourself and your resources, making a plan and carrying it out)

	1	2	3	4	5

(continued)

TABLE 9.1. (CONTINUED)

32. Seeking advice (through books or asking others for guidance)

    1   2   3   4   5

33. Asserting yourself (standing up for yourself)

    1   2   3   4   5

34. Brainstorming a new plan (generating all possible suggestions or solutions)

    1   2   3   4   5

35. Setting new goals (writing a realistic and flexible "next steps" approach)

    1   2   3   4   5

36. Applying knowledge of the transition process (recognizing that all change requires adaptation and time to adjust)

    1   2   3   4   5

37. Developing rituals (creating a meaningful way to acknowledge your transition)

    1   2   3   4   5

38. Making positive comparisons (counting your blessings, comparing your situation to those less fortunate)

    1   2   3   4   5

39. Rearranging priorities (defining other areas of your life as more important)

    1   2   3   4   5

40. Reappraising, relabeling, reframing (redefining the transition in a more positive way)

    1   2   3   4   5

41. Ignoring selectively (playing down bad parts and playing up good ones)

    1   2   3   4   5

42. Denying (delaying facing the facts for a short time)

    1   2   3   4   5

43. Engaging in humor (improving your laugh life)

      1   2   3   4   5

44. Being spiritual (reflecting through prayer, meditation, or solitude)

      1   2   3   4   5

45. Positive self-talking (confirming your belief in yourself through verbal affirmations)

      1   2   3   4   5

46. Imaging desired outcome (seeing yourself where you want to be)

      1   2   3   4   5

47. Being mindful (able to focus on what needs to be done)

      1   2   3   4   5

48. Balancing your work, family, and leisure roles (able to devote time to all aspects of your life)

      1   2   3   4   5

49. Playing (allowing the child within to emerge and have fun)

      1   2   3   4   5

50. Using relaxation skills (controlling physical reactions to stressful situations through relaxation tapes, biofeedback, muscle relaxation, and/or visualization)

      1   2   3   4   5

51. Expressing emotions (letting off steam through crying, yelling, or vigorous physical activity)

      1   2   3   4   5

52. Engaging in physical activity (walking, running, tennis, or exercise of any kind)

      1   2   3   4   5

53. Participating in counseling, therapy, or support groups (working with a professional to help you manage stress, joining a support group with people experiencing a similar situation)

      1   2   3   4   5

(continued)

TABLE 9.1. (*CONTINUED*)

54. Managing your time (spending time in activities that are important to you)

       1   2   3   4   5

55. Doing nothing (consciously deciding to take no action—just sitting tight to see what happens)

       1   2   3   4   5

56. Using a range of strategies (knowing there is not one magic strategy but several that may help you cope)

       1   2   3   4   5

STOP HERE.

Add the numbers you have circled for items 30–56, and write the sum here: _____

Interpreting Your Scores

After completing the Transition Guide Questionnaire, total the scores you assigned to items in each section. Enter the score numbers under each factor: *Situation, Self, Supports,* and *Strategies.*

Write your *Situation* total score here _____
Items 1–10 Possible score range 10–50

Write your *Self* total score here _____
Items 11–20 Possible score range 10–50

Write your *Supports* total score here _____
Items 21–29 Possible score range 9–45

Write your *Strategies* total score here _____
Items 30–56 Possible score range 27–135

TABLE 9.2.   YOUR TRANSITION COPING RESOURCES

	Your Situation	Your Self	Your Supports	Your Strategies
HIGH				
Your coping resources	50	50	45	135
are strong	49	49	44	132
	48	49	43	129
	47	47	42	126
	46	46	41	123
	45	45	40	125
	44	44	39	120
	43	43	38	117
	42	42	37	114
	41	41	36	111
	40	40	35	108
	39	39	34	105
	38	38		102
				99
MEDIUM				
Your coping resources	37	37	33	98
are moderate	36	36	32	96
	35	35	31	93
	34	34	30	90
	33	33	29	87
	32	32	28	84
	31	31	27	81
	30	30	26	78
	29	29	25	75
	28	28	24	72
	27	27	23	69
	26	26	22	66
	25	25	21	63
	24	24		
	23	23		

(*continued*)

TABLE 9.2.   (CONTINUED)

	Your Situation	Your Self	Your Supports	Your Strategies
LOW				
You may need to develop	22	22	20	62
new strategies for	21	21	19	60
coping with these	20	20	18	57
areas	19	19	17	54
	18	18	16	51
	17	17	15	48
	16	16	14	45
	15	15	13	42
	14	14	12	39
	13	13	11	36
	12	12	10	33
	11	11	9	30
	10	10		27

Next mark each score in the appropriate column on table 9.2.

PUTTING THE PARTS TOGETHER

Let's see how the whole concept works. Think of two people faced with the same transition—for example, a woman and a man whose jobs are in jeopardy—and look at the differences in their readiness for change. For the woman, the *Situation* occurs at a good time. She has been thinking of returning to school to get a degree. She has been waiting for a reason to leave her job. In terms of her inner resources, she generally copes well and is able to tell herself, "It could be worse. I won't go hungry." In terms of her external resources, she has a supportive husband who will provide financial backing, and she has several very supportive friends. We can see that the balance of her resources far outweigh her deficits.

The man whose job is in jeopardy is a single parent with three children, two of whom want to go to college. His steady income is essential. He has just gone through a painful divorce, and his ex-wife is mentally ill. His *Situation* is difficult, his coping *Strategies* are limited at this time, and his *Support* system is practically nil. His ability to deal with a job change is very low.

Another example might be two people making geographical moves from one country to another. One person may have no support from family members, while another person may have a problem finding a new job. Adapting to a new culture brings a new set of challenges that take time to adjust to and require more than one coping strategy.

Because everyone's transition is unique, each individual's *Strategy* for working through change may be different.

Step One—Approach Change

Identify the way your transition has changed your life. Transitions can be either positive or negative—both of which can be stressful. If the transition has altered your life in significant ways, you need to expand your resources for coping.

In addition, it is important to realize that your reactions to transitions change over time. If you are at the beginning of the transition, you will think of little else. If you are in the middle of it, you might be confused as you try to figure out new directions. If you have completed the process, you will have established a new focus. Remember that even if the transition is positive, you can still have the feelings of loss as you leave familiar roles and try to develop new roles.

Step Two—Take Stock of Your Resources for Managing Changes—Your 4 S's

What Is Your *Situation* (How you see the Transition)? As you contemplate making a change or weathering a change, think about the

Situation. Is it positive? Negative? Expected? Unexpected? Does the transition come at the worst or best possible time? Are you dealing with more than one life event? Is it a move up or a move down? Have you had previous experience with similar transitions?

What About Your *Self* (Who You Are)? Do you have the inner strength to deal with it? Do you feel overwhelmed or challenged? Do you have an optimistic outlook? How well do you know yourself?

What Are Your *Supports* (What Help You Have from Others)? Do you have the external resources and support to deal with change? Do you have support from family, close friends, and coworkers? Do you have support networks in your community and on the job? Is there a match between what you need and what you have?

What Are Your *Strategies* (How You Cope)? Do you know when to take action? Do you know when to refrain from taking direct action? Can you change the way you see things? How do you manage your reactions to the transition? Do you use a variety of coping *Strategies?*

Step Three—Take Charge of the Transition

This is your chance to turn the tide by considering which suggestions listed below would be most appropriate for improving each of your "low" areas. When you work on your own plan you may also come up with other ideas that are not listed. Then, prioritize the strategies appropriate for you—ones that have a good chance of success. Even a small degree of change can increase your sense of control and well-being.

To Strengthen Your Situation—Think of ways you can seek advice, negotiate, take optimistic action, and assert yourself;

- Reframe the transition by viewing it in a different way;
- Try to see a positive outcome to the transition;
- Read a book about your situation to shed new light on options.

To Strengthen Your Self—Try to see yourself in a different light;

- Know that feelings of loss and sadness are normal and that transitions take time to integrate;
- View the transition as strengthening your ability to cope;
- Practice affirming yourself;
- Read a self-help book for inspiration and insight.

To Strengthen Your Support—Think about what you need, and how you can get it;

- Practice asking for support—it gets easier;
- Join a support group with others who are going through a similar transition;
- Brainstorm ways to create more support.

To Strengthen Your Strategies—Think about what strategies you usually use. You may find yourself using the same few strategies again and again. Are these strategies working? Think about new strategies that might help you.

Review your coping skills. Select three new strategies that will help you achieve balance in your life. Taking positive action in one area of your life, perhaps by adding a walk or a relaxation exercise to your daily routine, frequently has a ripple effect.

MOVING FORWARD—YOUR ACTION PLAN

List three steps you will take to raise your low or medium scores:

1. _____

_____

_____

2. _____

_____

_____

3. _____

_____

_____

Finally, take action on your plan and remember . . . Transition Works!

AFTERWORD:
MY FINAL WORD:
MAKE THE MOST WITH
WHAT YOU HAVE

The following story about the famous violinist Itzhak Perlman says it all. According to a report in the *Houston Chronicle* Perlman was playing in a concert when one of the strings on his violin snapped. "If you have ever been to a Perlman concert, you know that getting on stage is no small achievement for him. He was stricken with polio as a child. To see him walk across the stage one step at a time, painfully and slowly, is an awesome sight. Just as he finished the first few bars, one of the strings on his violin broke. You could hear it snap—it went off like gunfire across the room . . . he waited a moment, closed his eyes, and then signaled the conductor to begin again. The orchestra began, and he played . . . with such passion and such power. Of course, anyone knows that it is impossible to play a symphonic work with just three strings. I know that, and you know that, but that night, Itzhak Perlman refused to know that. . . . When he finished, there was an awesome silence. . . . And then people rose and cheered." When the applause died down, these words were Perlman's response: 'You know, sometimes it is the artist's task to find out how much music you can still make with what you have left.'"

Jack Riemer, the author of the article, concluded: "So, perhaps our task in this shaky, fast-changing, bewildering world . . . is to make music, at first with all that we have, and then, when that is no longer possible, to make music with what we have left."[1]

So let's all keep making music.

NOTES

PREFACE

1. Phyllis Moen and Vivian Fields, "Midcourse in the United States: Does Unpaid Community Participation Replace Paid Work?" *Aging International* 27(3): 21–48.

CHAPTER 2. TRANSITIONS: THEIR INFINITE VARIETY

1. Nancy K. Schlossberg and Susan P. Robinson, *Going to Plan B: How You Can Cope, Regroup, and Start Your Life on a New Path* (New York: Simon & Schuster, 1996).
2. Gunhild O. Hagestad, "The Social Meanings of Age," in *The Adult Years: Continuity and Change*, ed. N. K. Schlossberg et al. (Owings Mills, Md.: International University Consortium, 1985).

CHAPTER 3. TAKING STOCK OF YOUR *SITUATION*

1. Richard Lazarus and Susan Folkman, *Stress, Appraisal, and Coping* (New York: Springer, 1984).
2. Nancy K. Schlossberg and Zandy B. Leibowitz, "Organizational Support Systems as Buffers to Job Loss," *Journal of Vocational Behavior* 18 (1980): 204–17.

3. Christopher Peterson and Martin Seligman, "Causal Explanations as a Risk Factor for Depression: Theory and Evidence," *Psychological Review* 91 (1984): 347–74.

4. Marylu McEwen, Susan Komives, and Nancy Schlossberg, *Departing the College Presidency: Voices of Women and Men in Transition* (College Park, MD: University of Maryland, 1988).

5. Bernice L. Neugarten, "Time, Age, and the Life Cycle," *American Journal of Psychiatry* 136 (1979): 887–94.

6. Judith Rodin and C. Timko, "Sense of Control, Aging, and Health," in *Aging Health and Behavior*, ed. M. G. Fry, R. P. Abeles, and D. D. Lipman, 174–206. (Newbury Park, CA: Sage Publications, 1992).

7. Robert Seidenberg, *Corporate Wives: Corporate Casualties* (New York: AmCom Division of American Management Association, 1973).

CHAPTER 4. TAKING STOCK OF YOUR *SELF* AND YOUR *SUPPORTS*

1. George E. Vaillant, *The Wisdom of the Ego* (Cambridge, MA: Harvard University Press, 1993).

2. S. R. Maddi, "The Story of Hardiness: Twenty Years of Theorizing, Research, and Practice," *Consulting Psychology Journal: Practice and Research* 54, no. 3 (2002): 174.

3. Shelley Taylor, "Adjustment to Threatening Events: A Theory of Cognitive Adaptation," quoted in *APA News Release* (December 1, 1983).

4. Grace Baruch, Rosalind Barnett, and Caryl Rivers, *Lifeprints: New Patterns of Love and Work for Today's Women* (New York: New American Library, 1983).

5. Martin Seligman, *Learned Optimism* (New York: Alfred A. Knopf, 1991).

6. Christopher Peterson and Martin Seligman, "Causal Explanations as a Risk Factor for Depression: Theory and Evidence," *Psychological Review* 91 (1984): 3347–74.

7. D. Kiersey and M. Bates, *Please Understand Me: Character and Temperament Types* (Del Mar, CA: Prometheus Nemesis Book Company, 1984).

8. Richard Lazarus and Susan Folkman, *Stress, Appraisal, and Coping* (New York: Springer, 1984), 19.

9. Robert Kahn and T. C. Antonucci, "Convoys Over the Life Course: Attachment, Roles, and Social Support," in *Lifespan Development and Behavior*, vol. 3, ed. P. B. Baltes and O. G. Brim, Jr., 253–86 (New York: Academic Press, 1980).

10. Gunhild O. Hagestad, "Vertical Bonds: Intergenerational Relationships," in *The Adult Years: Continuity and Change*, ed. N. K. Schlossberg et al. (Owings Mills, Md.: International University Consortium, 1985).

11. Lillian Rubin, *Just Friends: The Role of Friendship in our Lives* (New York: Harper & Row, 1985).

12. S. E. Taylor, L. C. Klein, B. P. Lewis, T. L. Gruenewald, R. A. R. Gurung, and J. A. Updegraff, "Female Responses to Stress: Tend and Befriend, Not Fight or Flight," *Psychological Review* 107, no. 3 (2000): 411–29.

13. Hagestad, "Vertical Bonds," 133–66.

14. Kahn and Antonucci, "Convoys Over the Life Course," 273.

CHAPTER 5. TAKING STOCK OF YOUR *STRATEGIES*

1. Leonard Pearlin and Carmi Schooler, "The Structure of Coping," *Journal of Health and Human Behavior* 19 (1978): 2–21

2. Lazarus and Folkman, *Stress, Appraisal, and Coping.* (New York: Springer, 1984).

3. Ivan Charner and Nancy Schlossberg, "Variations by the Theme: The Life Transitions of Clerical Workers," *Vocational Guidance Quarterly* 34 (1986): 212–24.

4. Gerard I. Nierenberg, *Fundamentals of Negotiating* (New York: Hawthorn Books, 1973).

5. Psychology Matters: American Psychology Association website: at http://psychologymatters.apa.org

6. Salvatore Maddi and Deborah Khoshaba, "The Story of Hardiness: Twenty Years of Theorizing, Research, and Practice," *Consulting Psychology Journal: Practice and Research* 54, no. 3 (2002): 173–85.

7. Bernice Neugarten. "Time, Age, and the Life Cycle," *American Journal of Psychiatry* 136 (1979): 887–94.

8. Barbara Myerhoff, Film, "Rites of Renewal," Owings Mills, MD: International University Consortium and Ohio University (1985). Also see "Rites and Signs of Ripening and Intertwining of Ritual, Time and Growing Older," in *Age and Anthropological Theory*, eds. D. Kertzer and J. Keith, 305–330 (Ithaca, N.Y.: Cornell University Press, 1984).

9. Shelley Taylor, *Positive Illusions* (New York: Basic Books, 1989).

10. Robert Enright, *Forgiveness Is a Choice: A Step-by-Step Process for Resolving Anger and Restoring Hope* (Washington, DC: American Psychological Association, 2001).

11. George Vaillant, *Adaptation to Life* (Boston: Little, Brown, 1977).

12. R. S. Lazarus, *Emotion and Adaptation* (Oxford: Oxford University Press, 1991), 82.

13. Vaillant, *Adaptation to Life*, see 5–18.

CHAPTER 6: YOUR ACTION PLAN FOR MASTERING CHANGE

1. Nancy K. Schlossberg, *Retire Smart, Retire Happy: Finding Your True Path in Life* (Washington, DC: American Psychological Association, 2004).

CHAPTER 7. TAKING CHARGE OF YOUR NON-EVENT TRANSITIONS

1. This chapter was based on studies done at the University of Maryland and the trade book by Nancy K. Schlossberg and Susan Robinson, *Going to Plan B: How You Can Cope, Regroup, and Start Your Life on a New Path* (New York: Simon & Schuster, A Fireside Book, 1996).

2. Kenneth Doka, *Disenfranchised Grief* (New York: Lexington Books, 1989).

3. Myerhoff, "Rites of Renewal" and "Rites and Signs of Ripening."

4. "Rites of Independence: New Ceremonies for New People," *Ms.* Magazine, (September 1984).

5. Lazarus and Folkman, *Stress, Appraisal, and Coping.*

CHAPTER 8. TAKING CHARGE OF YOUR WORK/LIFE TRANSITIONS

1. Stephanie Kay, personal communication (2005).

2. Phyllis Moen and Patricia Roehling, *The Career Mystique: Cracks in the American Dream* (Lanham, MD: Rowman & Littlefield, 2005), 7, 10.

3. Moen and Roehling, *Career Mystique*, 10.

4. Meryl Louis, "Surprise and Sense Making: What Newcomers Experience in Entering Unfamiliar Organizational Settings," *Administrative Science Quarterly* 25 (June 1980): 7.

5. Lauren Picker, "And Now, the Hard Part," *Newsweek*, April 25, 2005, 46.

6. J. Gross, "It's Cold on Mars," *New York Times*, July 22, 2004, D1, D8.

7. Judith Bardwick, *Plateauing* (New York: AMACOM, 1986).

8. Louis, "Surprise and Sense Making," 74.

CHAPTER 9. IT'S YOUR TURN NOW

1. Stephanie Kay and Nancy K. Schlossberg, *The Transition Guide and Questionnaire* (2006). Available by contacting TransitionWorks, Inc., at www.transitionguide.com, or e-mail info@transitionguide.com. TransitionWorks has granted permission to reproduce this Guide but it cannot be copied and used, other than in this book.

AFTERWORD: MY FINAL WORD

1. Jack Riemer, *Houston Chronicle*, November 18, 1995.

ABOUT THE AUTHOR

Nancy K. Schlossberg is the author of eight books. She is copresident of TransitionWorks, a consulting firm, and professor emerita at the College of Education, University of Maryland, College Park. She served as president of the National Career Development Association and has been honored for her work by the American Psychological Association and the American Counseling Association. Dr. Schlossberg's work was showcased on page one of *USA Today* and quoted in the *New York Times*, the *St. Petersburg Times*, the *Wall Street Journal*, and Cleveland's *Plain Dealer*. A frequent guest on radio and TV, she has appeared on PBS's *In the Prime*, *CBS Evening News*, and *CBS This Morning*. She and her book are the focus of a 90-minute PBS pledge special, "Retire Smart, Retire Happy."

Made in the USA
Monee, IL
14 November 2023

46563384R00127